Contents

GOT SOME CRUST MACARONI AND CHEESE

Servings: 12 | Prep: 20m | Cooks: 55m | Total: 1h15m

NUTRITION FACTS

Calories: 286 | Carbohydrates: 23.2g | Fat: 15.5g | Protein: 13.1g | Cholesterol: 45mg

INGREDIENTS

- 2 cups elbow macaroni
- 1/4 teaspoon hot pepper sauce (such as Tabasco)
- 1/4 cup butter, divided
- 1 teaspoon prepared yellow mustard
- 1 small onion, chopped
- 2 cups shredded Cheddar cheese
- 2 tablespoons all-purpose flour
- 1/4 cup grated Parmesan cheese
- 1 1/2 cups milk
- 1 cup shredded Cheddar cheese
- 1 teaspoon salt
- 1/4 cup grated Parmesan cheese
- 1 teaspoon white pepper
- 1 cup dry bread crumbs
- 1 teaspoon Worcestershire sauce

DIRECTIONS

1. Preheat an oven to 350 degrees F (175 degrees C). Grease a 9x13 inch glass baking dish.
2. Fill a large pot with lightly salted water and bring to a rolling boil over high heat. Once the water is boiling, stir in the macaroni, and return to a boil. Cook the pasta uncovered, stirring occasionally, until the pasta has cooked through, but is still firm to the bite, about 8 minutes. Drain and mix with half of the butter.
3. While the macaroni is boiling, melt the remaining butter in a saucepan over medium heat. Stir in the onions, and cook until the onions begin to soften, about 3 minutes. Stir in the flour, and cook 5 minutes longer. Add the milk and bring to a simmer, stirring frequently. Cook and stir until the milk has thickened, about 10 minutes. Once thick and smooth, stir in the salt, white pepper, Worcestershire sauce, hot pepper sauce, mustard, 2 cups of Cheddar cheese, and 1/4 cup of Parmesan cheese. Stir until the cheeses have melted, then stir in the macaroni until evenly coated. Scrape into the prepared baking dish, and smooth the top. Toss the remaining 1 cup Cheddar cheese and 1/4 cup Parmesan cheese with the dry bread crumbs in a mixing bowl. Sprinkle evenly over the top of the macaroni.
4. Bake in the preheated oven until the macaroni is hot and the crust is golden brown, about 30 minutes.

INSTANT POT MAC AND CHEESE WITH HAM AND PEAS

Servings: 6 | Prep: 25m | Cooks: 14m | Total: 44m | Additional: 5m

NUTRITION FACTS

Calories: 607 | Carbohydrates: 65.4g | Fat: 22.9g | Protein: 33.3g | Cholesterol: 67mg

INGREDIENTS

- 4 cups water
- 2 tablespoons unsalted butter
- 1 (16 ounce) package elbow macaroni
- 2 cups shredded 2% milk Cheddar cheese (such as Kraft)
- 1 teaspoon dry mustard powder (such as Colman's)
- 1 cup shredded Monterey Jack cheese
- 1 teaspoon salt
- 1 cup diced cooked ham
- 1 teaspoon hot sauce (optional)
- 1/2 cup frozen peas, defrosted
- 1 (12 fluid ounce) can evaporated milk
- salt and ground black pepper to taste
- 1/3 cup whole milk

DIRECTIONS

1. Combine water, elbow macaroni, mustard powder, salt, and hot sauce in an electric pressure cooker (such as Instant Pot). Close and lock the lid. Set to high pressure according to manufacturer's instructions and cook for 4 minutes. Allow up to 10 minutes for pressure to build.
2. Release pressure carefully using the quick-release method according to manufacturer's instructions, about 5 minutes. Unlock and remove lid. Switch to Low Saute function by pressing Saute once and Adjust twice. Stir macaroni to separate any clumps.
3. Stir evaporated milk, milk, and butter into the pot. Add Cheddar cheese and Monterey Jack cheese gradually, stirring constantly until melted. Stir in ham and peas. Season with salt and pepper.

BUFFALO CHICKEN MAC AND CHEESE

Servings: 8 | Prep: 15m | Cooks: 20m | Total: 35m

NUTRITION FACTS

Calories: 781 | Carbohydrates: 51.7g | Fat: 41.9g | Protein: 47.3g | Cholesterol: 157mg

INGREDIENTS

- 1 (16 ounce) package elbow macaroni

- 1 pinch ground black pepper
- 1 rotisserie-roasted chicken
- 2 cups shredded Cheddar cheese
- 6 tablespoons butter
- 2 cups shredded Monterey Jack cheese
- 6 tablespoons all-purpose flour
- 1/2 cup hot sauce (such as Frank's Redhot), or more to taste
- 3 cups milk
- 1/2 cup crumbled gorgonzola cheese

DIRECTIONS

1. Bring a large pot of lightly salted water to a boil. Cook macaroni in the boiling water, stirring occasionally until tender yet firm to the bite, 8 minutes. Drain.
2. Cut wings and legs off rotisserie chicken. Skin and bone wings and legs; chop or shred dark meat into bite-size pieces.
3. Melt butter in a large Dutch oven over medium heat. Whisk in flour gradually until a thick paste forms. Cook until golden, about 1 minute. Pour in milk, whisking constantly, until thickened and bubbling, about 5 minutes. Continue to cook until sauce is smooth, about 1 minute more. Reduce heat and season sauce with black pepper.
4. Stir Cheddar and Monterey Jack cheese into the sauce until melted and combined. Stir in hot sauce, adjusting to reach desired level of spiciness. Add blue cheese, chicken, and macaroni; mix well to combine.

CAULIFLOWER MAC-N-CHEESE
Servings: 4 | Prep: 10m | Cooks: 20m | Total: 30m

NUTRITION FACTS

Calories: 471 | Carbohydrates: 34.3g | Fat: 28.5g | Protein: 19.3g | Cholesterol: 78mg

INGREDIENTS

- 1 1/2 cups elbow macaroni
- 1/2 cup milk
- 1/2 cup cauliflower florets
- 1 1/2 cups shredded Cheddar cheese
- cooking spray
- 1/2 (8 ounce) package cream cheese
- 1 tablespoon olive oil
- 1/2 teaspoon salt
- 1 tablespoon all-purpose flour
- 1/8 teaspoon ground black pepper

DIRECTIONS

1. Bring a large pot of lightly salted water to a boil. Cook elbow macaroni in the boiling water, stirring occasionally until tender yet firm to the bite, 8 minutes. Drain.
2. Place a steamer insert into a saucepan and fill with water to just below the bottom of the steamer. Bring water to a boil. Add cauliflower, cover, and steam until tender, 5 to 6 minutes. Place cauliflower in a blender or food processor; blend until smooth.
3. Coat a large saucepan with non-stick cooking spray; place over medium heat. Add oil and flour; cook, stirring constantly, until a thick paste forms, 1 to 2 minutes. Add milk; cook and stir until mixture thickens, 3 to 4 minutes.
4. Mix cauliflower, Cheddar cheese, cream cheese, salt, and pepper into milk mixture; stir until sauce is smooth. Fold macaroni into sauce.

GLUTEN-FREE MAC-N-CHEESE

Servings: 6 | Prep: 10m | Cooks: 20m | Total: 30m

NUTRITION FACTS

Calories: 620 | Carbohydrates: 57.9g | Fat: 35.6g | Protein: 19g | Cholesterol: 104mg

INGREDIENTS

- 12 ounces gluten-free pasta (such as Barilla)
- 1 (12 fluid ounce) can evaporated milk
- 6 tablespoons butter
- 2 cups shredded Cheddar cheese
- 1/2 onion, chopped
- 1/3 cup mascarpone cheese
- 1/4 cup potato starch
- 3 dashes hot sauce (such as Tabasco) (optional)

DIRECTIONS

1. Bring a large pot of lightly salted water to a boil. Cook pasta in the boiling water, stirring occasionally until tender yet firm to the bite, about 7 minutes. Drain and reserve 1/2 cup cooking liquid. Transfer pasta to a serving bowl.
2. Melt butter in a saucepan over medium heat; add onion and cook until translucent, about 3 minutes. Stir potato starch into onion mixture until dissolved, about 1 minute. Slowly pour evaporated milk into onion mixture and stir constantly. Bring sauce to a simmer and remove saucepan from heat.
3. Stir Cheddar cheese, mascarpone cheese, and hot sauce into sauce until smooth, adding the reserved pasta cooking liquid if needed to thin the sauce. The cheese sauce should be the consistency of gravy.
4. Mix cheese sauce into pasta and serve while warm and gooey.

WISCONSIN FIVE-CHEESE BAKE

Servings: 12 | Prep: 10m | Cooks: 15m | Total: 25m

NUTRITION FACTS

Calories: 328 | Carbohydrates: 30.8g | Fat: 15.4g | Protein: 16g | Cholesterol: 46mg

INGREDIENTS

- 1 (16 ounce) package elbow macaroni
- 1/2 cup sour cream
- 1 cup shredded mozzarella cheese
- 1/2 cup heavy cream
- 1 cup shredded Swiss cheese
- 1 tablespoon chopped fresh parsley
- 1 cup grated Parmesan cheese
- 1/2 teaspoon dried Italian seasoning
- 1 cup shredded provolone cheese
- 1/2 teaspoon garlic salt
- 1/2 cup ricotta cheese

DIRECTIONS

1. Preheat the oven to 400 degrees F (200 degrees C). Lightly grease a 9x13 inch baking dish. Bring a large pot of lightly salted water to a boil. Add macaroni, and cook until tender, 6 to 8 minutes. Drain.
2. In a large bowl, toss together the mozzarella cheese, Swiss cheese, Parmesan cheese and Provolone cheese. Remove about 1/2 cup for topping and set aside. In a separate bowl, stir together the ricotta cheese, sour cream and heavy cream. Season with parsley, Italian seasoning and garlic salt.
3. Pour the ricotta cheese mixture and drained macaroni into the bowl with the cheeses and toss lightly. Do not mix too thoroughly, it's better left messy. Pour into the prepared baking dish. Sprinkle the reserved cheese over the top.
4. Bake in the preheated oven until cheese is melted, about 10 minutes, then turn the oven to broil. Broil for about 5 minutes to brown the top.

KICKED UP MAC AND CHEESE

Servings: 8 | Prep: 30m | Cooks: 40m | Total: 1h10m

NUTRITION FACTS

Calories: 352 | Carbohydrates: 19.6g | Fat: 23.3g | Protein: 16.4g | Cholesterol: 69mg

INGREDIENTS

- 1 1/2 cups rotelle pasta

- 3 teaspoons hot pepper sauce
- 4 tablespoons butter, divided
- 1 cup shredded pepperjack cheese
- 1/4 cup all-purpose flour
- 1 1/2 cups shredded sharp Cheddar cheese
- 3 cups whole milk
- 1/2 cup grated Parmesan cheese
- 1 teaspoon dry mustard
- 1/3 cup dry bread crumbs
- 3/4 teaspoon salt
- 2 teaspoons chili powder
- 1/2 teaspoon ground white pepper

DIRECTIONS

1. Preheat oven to 375 degrees F (190 degrees C).
2. Bring a large pot of lightly salted water to a boil. Add pasta and cook for 8 to 10 minutes or until al dente; drain.
3. In a large saucepan over medium heat, melt 2 tablespoons butter. Whisk in flour and cook, stirring, 1 minute. A little at a time, whisk in milk, mustard, salt, pepper and hot sauce. Bring to a gentle boil, stirring constantly. Boil 1 minute, then remove from heat and whisk in pepperjack, Cheddar and Parmesan until smooth. Stir in cooked pasta and pour into shallow 2 quart baking dish.
4. Melt remaining 2 tablespoons butter. Stir in bread crumbs and chili powder. Sprinkle over macaroni mixture.
5. Bake in preheated oven 30 minutes. Let stand 10 minutes before serving.

BAKED HOMEMADE MACARONI AND CHEESE

Servings: 6 | Prep: 15m | Cooks: 1h | Total: 1h15m

NUTRITION FACTS

Calories: 810 | Carbohydrates: 57.3g | Fat: 49.9g | Protein: 32.4g | Cholesterol: 133mg

INGREDIENTS

- 2 1/2 cups elbow macaroni
- 4 cups milk
- 1/4 cup butter
- 1 pound shredded Cheddar cheese
- 1/4 cup all-purpose flour
- 1/4 cup butter, melted
- 1/2 teaspoon salt
- 1 sleeve buttery round crackers, crushed

DIRECTIONS

1. Preheat the oven to 350 degrees F (175 degrees C).
2. Fill a large pot with lightly salted water and bring to a boil over high heat. Stir in the macaroni, and cook uncovered, stirring occasionally, until the pasta has cooked through, but is still firm to the bite, about 8 minutes. Drain well.
3. Melt 1/4 cup butter in a large saucepan over medium heat. Stir in flour and salt. Cook, stirring constantly, for 2 minutes. Whisk in milk and simmer, stirring frequently, until mixture thickens slightly, about 5 minutes.
4. Turn off heat and stir in Cheddar cheese until the cheese is melted. Add the macaroni and stir to coat. Pour the mixture into a 9x13-inch baking dish. Mix the 1/4 remaining cup melted butter and crushed crackers together in a bowl; scatter the cracker mixture evenly over the macaroni mixture.
5. Bake in preheated oven until golden brown on top, about 45 minutes.

EASY MAC AND CHEESE MUFFINS

Servings: 12 | Prep: 15m | Cooks: 40m | Total: 55m

NUTRITION FACTS

Calories: 208 | Carbohydrates: 18g | Fat: 10g | Protein: 11.1g | Cholesterol: 44mg

INGREDIENTS

- 2 cups uncooked elbow macaroni
- 1 1/2 cups shredded mozzarella cheese
- 1 tablespoon butter
- 1/2 cup seasoned dry bread crumbs
- 1 egg, beaten
- 2 teaspoons olive oil
- 1 cup milk
- 1/2 teaspoon salt
- 1 1/2 cups shredded sharp Cheddar cheese

DIRECTIONS

1. Preheat the oven to 350 degrees F (175 degrees C). Grease a muffin tin with nonstick cooking spray. In a small bowl, stir together the bread crumbs, olive oil and salt; set aside.
2. Bring a large pot of lightly salted water to a boil. Add the macaroni and cook for about 8 minutes, it should still be a little bit firm. Remove from the heat, drain and return to the pan; stir in the butter and egg until pasta is evenly coated. Reserve 1/2 cup of sharp Cheddar cheese and stir the remaining Cheddar cheese, milk and mozzarella cheese into the pasta. Spoon into the prepared muffin tin. Sprinkle the reserved cheese and the bread crumb mixture over the tops.

3. Bake for 30 minutes in the preheated oven, or until the topping is nicely browned. Allow the muffins to cool for a few minutes before removing from the pan. This will allow the cheese to set and they will hold their muffin shape.

CHUCK'S FAVORITE MAC AND CHEESE

Servings: 6 | Prep: 10m | Cooks: 45m | Total: 55m

NUTRITION FACTS

Calories: 591 | Carbohydrates: 45.5g | Fat: 33.3g | Protein: 26.8g | Cholesterol: 88mg

INGREDIENTS

- 1 (8 ounce) package elbow macaroni
- 1/4 cup grated Parmesan cheese
- 1 (8 ounce) package shredded sharp Cheddar cheese
- salt and pepper to taste
- 1 (12 ounce) container small curd cottage cheese
- 1 cup dry bread crumbs
- 1 (8 ounce) container sour cream
- 1/4 cup butter, melted

DIRECTIONS

1. Preheat oven to 350 degrees F (175 degrees C). Bring a large pot of lightly salted water to a boil, add pasta, and cook until done; drain.
2. In 9x13 inch baking dish, stir together macaroni, shredded Cheddar cheese, cottage cheese, sour cream, Parmesan cheese, salt and pepper. In a small bowl, mix together bread crumbs and melted butter. Sprinkle topping over macaroni mixture.
3. Bake 30 to 35 minutes, or until top is golden.

HOMEMADE MAC AND CHEESE

Servings: 4 | Prep: 20m | Cooks: 30m | Total: 50m

NUTRITION FACTS

Calories: 858 | Carbohydrates: 66.7g | Fat: 48.7g | Protein: 37.7g | Cholesterol: 142mg

INGREDIENTS

- 8 ounces uncooked elbow macaroni
- 2 1/2 tablespoons all-purpose flour
- 2 cups shredded sharp Cheddar cheese

- 2 tablespoons butter
- 1/2 cup grated Parmesan cheese
- 1/2 cup bread crumbs
- 3 cups milk
- 1 pinch paprika
- 1/4 cup butter

DIRECTIONS

1. Cook macaroni according to the package directions. Drain.
2. In a saucepan, melt butter or margarine over medium heat. Stir in enough flour to make a roux. Add milk to roux slowly, stirring constantly. Stir in cheeses, and cook over low heat until cheese is melted and the sauce is a little thick. Put macaroni in large casserole dish, and pour sauce over macaroni. Stir well.
3. Melt butter or margarine in a skillet over medium heat. Add breadcrumbs and brown. Spread over the macaroni and cheese to cover. Sprinkle with a little paprika.
4. Bake at 350 degrees F (175 degrees C) for 30 minutes. Serve.

MACARONI AND CHEESE

Servings: 6 | Prep: 15m | Cooks: 45m | Total: 1h

NUTRITION FACTS

Calories: 695 | Carbohydrates: 72.8g | Fat: 32.3g | Protein: 29.4g | Cholesterol: 95mg

INGREDIENTS

- 1 (16 ounce) package elbow macaroni
- 1 pinch ground nutmeg
- 1/4 cup butter
- 1/4 teaspoon Worcestershire sauce
- 1/4 cup all-purpose flour
- 1 teaspoon salt
- 1/4 teaspoon dried thyme
- 3 cups shredded sharp Cheddar cheese, divided
- 1/4 teaspoon cayenne pepper
- 1 teaspoon Dijon mustard
- 1/8 teaspoon white pepper
- 1/2 cup panko bread crumbs
- 3 cups milk
- 1 tablespoon butter, melted

DIRECTIONS

1. Preheat oven to 400 degrees F (200 degrees C).
2. Fill a large pot with lightly salted water and bring to a rolling boil over high heat. Once the water is boiling, stir in the macaroni, and return to a boil. Cook the pasta uncovered, stirring occasionally, until the pasta is cooked through but still slightly firm, about 8 minutes. Drain well.
3. Melt 1/4 cup butter in a large saucepan over medium heat. When the butter starts to foam and bubble, stir in the flour; cook on medium heat until flour just begins to turn pale yellow, 3 to 4 minutes. Add thyme, cayenne pepper, and white pepper; cook and stir another minute, then whisk in 1 cup of milk until smooth. Pour in remaining milk and whisk again. Bring the sauce just to a simmer.
4. Stir in nutmeg, Worcestershire sauce, and salt; simmer on medium-low heat until thickened, about 8 minutes, whisking often. Turn heat off, then add 2 1/4 cups of Cheddar cheese; stir until melted and combined. Add Dijon mustard.
5. Transfer the macaroni into a casserole dish, then pour in the cheese sauce; stir to thoroughly combine sauce with pasta. Mix panko bread crumbs and 1 tablespoon melted butter in a small bowl, and sprinkle crumbs on top of macaroni and cheese. Sprinkle remaining 3/4 cup of Cheddar cheese on top.
6. Bake in the preheated oven until bread crumbs and Cheddar cheese topping are golden brown, about 20 minutes.

MOUSE'S MACARONI AND CHEESE

Servings: 6 | Prep: 15m | Cooks: 35m | Total: 50m

NUTRITION FACTS

Calories: 463 | Carbohydrates: 34.2g | Fat: 25.9g | Protein: 23g | Cholesterol: 78mg

INGREDIENTS

- 1 1/2 cups uncooked elbow macaroni
- 2 cups milk
- 1/4 cup butter
- 8 ounces American cheese, cubed
- 2 tablespoons all-purpose flour
- 8 ounces processed cheese food (eg. Velveeta), cubed
- 1 teaspoon mustard powder
- 1/4 cup seasoned dry bread crumbs
- 1 teaspoon ground black pepper

DIRECTIONS

1. Preheat oven to 400 degrees F (205 degrees C). Butter a 1 1/2 quart casserole dish. Bring a saucepan of lightly salted water to a boil. Add macaroni, and cook until not quite done, about 6 minutes. Drain.

2. In a separate saucepan, melt the butter over medium heat. Blend in the flour, mustard powder, and pepper until smooth. Slowly stir in the milk, beating out any lumps. Add the American and processed cheeses, and stir constantly until the sauce is thick and smooth.
3. Drain noodles, and stir them into the cheese sauce. Transfer the mixture to the prepared casserole dish. Sprinkle bread crumbs over the top.
4. Cover the dish, and bake for 20 to 25 minutes, or until sauce is thick and bubbly.

MOM'S FAVORITE BAKED MAC AND CHEESE

Servings: 6 | Prep: 10m | Cooks: 45m | Total: 1h5m | Additional: 10m

NUTRITION FACTS

Calories: 561 | Carbohydrates: 36.5g | Fat: 33.3g | Protein: 28.3g | Cholesterol: 100mg

INGREDIENTS

- 2 tablespoons butter
- 1/2 teaspoon dry mustard
- 1/4 cup finely chopped onion
- 1/4 teaspoon ground black pepper
- 2 tablespoons all-purpose flour
- 1 (8 ounce) package elbow macaroni
- 2 cups milk
- 2 cups shredded sharp Cheddar cheese
- 3/4 teaspoon salt
- 1 (8 ounce) package processed American cheese, cut into strip

DIRECTIONS

1. Preheat oven to 350 degrees F (175 degrees C).
2. Melt butter in a medium saucepan over medium heat. Saute onion for 2 minutes. Stir in flour and cook 1 minute, stirring constantly. Stir in milk, salt, mustard and pepper; cook, stirring frequently, until mixture boils and thickens.
3. Meanwhile, bring a pot of lightly salted water to a boil. Add macaroni and cook for 8 to 10 minutes or until al dente; drain.
4. To the milk mixture add the Cheddar and American cheeses; stir until cheese melts. Combine macaroni and cheese sauce in a 2 quart baking dish; mix well.
5. Bake in preheated oven for 30 minutes, or until hot and bubbly. Let cool 10 minutes before serving.

OLD FASHIONED MAC AND CHEESE

Servings: 7 | Prep: 20m | Cooks: 45m | Total: 1h5m

NUTRITION FACTS

Calories: 401 | Carbohydrates: 29.1g | Fat: 23.3g | Protein: 18.5g | Cholesterol: 70mg

INGREDIENTS

- 2 cups uncooked elbow macaroni
- salt and pepper to taste
- 4 tablespoons butter
- 1/4 pound processed cheese food
- 2 tablespoons all-purpose flour
- 1/4 pound shredded Cheddar cheese
- 2 cups milk
- 1/4 pound shredded Swiss cheese
- 1/4 onion, minced

DIRECTIONS

1. Preheat oven to 350 degrees F (175 degrees C).
2. Prepare the elbow macaroni according to package directions.
3. Meanwhile, melt the butter in a small saucepan over medium high heat. Stir in the flour until a cream colored paste forms. Then pour in the milk and stir constantly until this comes to a hard boil, then stir for 1 more minute. Remove from heat and set aside.
4. When the macaroni is cooked, spread 1/2 of it into the bottom of a lightly greased 9x13-inch baking dish. Then layer 1/2 of the grated onion, 1/2 of the salt and pepper and 1/2 of each of the cheeses. Repeat this one more time: macaroni, onion, salt and pepper and cheeses, and then pour the reserved white sauce over all. Top off with small pats of butter to taste.
5. Cover and bake at 350 degrees F (175 degrees C) for 45 minutes.

HOME STYLE MACARONI AND CHEESE

Servings: 6 | Prep: 20m | Cooks: 20m | Total: 40m

NUTRITION FACTS

Calories: 641| Carbohydrates: 47g | Fat: 40.4g | Protein: 22.6g | Cholesterol: 118mg

INGREDIENTS

- 7 ounces macaroni
- 1/2 teaspoon black pepper
- 1/4 cup butter
- 2 teaspoons Dijon mustard
- 3 tablespoons all-purpose flour
- 2 cups shredded Cheddar cheese
- 2 cups milk
- 1 cup dry bread crumbs

- 1 (8 ounce) package cream cheese
- 2 tablespoons butter
- 1/2 teaspoon salt
- 2 tablespoons chopped fresh parsley

DIRECTIONS

1. Preheat oven to 400 degrees F (200 degrees C).
2. Bring a large pot of lightly salted water to a boil. Add macaroni pasta and cook for 8 to 10 minutes or until al dente; drain.
3. In a 3 quart saucepan over medium heat, melt butter and stir in flour. Cook for about 1 minute, until smooth and bubbly; stirring occasionally. Mix in milk, cream cheese, salt, pepper, and Dijon mustard. Continue cooking until sauce is thickened. Add cooked macaroni and Cheddar cheese.
4. Pour into 2 quart casserole dish. In small bowl mix together bread crumbs, butter and parsley; spread over macaroni and cheese. Bake for 15 to 20 minutes or until golden brown and heated through.

SIMPLE MACARONI AND CHEESE

Servings: 4 | Prep: 10m | Cooks: 20m | Total: 30m

NUTRITION FACTS

Calories: 630 | Carbohydrates: 55g | Fat: 33.6g | Protein: 26.5g | Cholesterol: 100mg

INGREDIENTS

- 1 (8 ounce) box elbow macaroni
- ground black pepper to taste
- 1/4 cup butter
- 2 cups milk
- 1/4 cup all-purpose flour
- 2 cups shredded Cheddar cheese
- 1/2 teaspoon salt

DIRECTIONS

1. Bring a large pot of lightly salted water to a boil. Cook elbow macaroni in the boiling water, stirring occasionally until cooked through but firm to the bite, 8 minutes. Drain.
2. Melt butter in a saucepan over medium heat; stir in flour, salt, and pepper until smooth, about 5 minutes. Slowly pour milk into butter-flour mixture while continuously stirring until mixture is smooth and bubbling, about 5 minutes. Add Cheddar cheese to milk mixture and stir until cheese is melted, 2 to 4 minutes.
3. Fold macaroni into cheese sauce until coated.

HAM AND CHEESE BOWTIES

Servings: 6 | Prep: 20m | Cooks: 25m | Total: 45m

NUTRITION FACTS

Calories: 508 | Carbohydrates: 36.5g | Fat: 29.7g | Protein: 24.2g | Cholesterol: 85mg

INGREDIENTS

- 8 ounces farfalle (bow tie) pasta
- 2 cups milk
- 1/4 cup butter
- 1/2 teaspoon prepared mustard
- 1 clove garlic, minced
- 2 1/2 cups shredded Colby cheese
- 1/4 cup all-purpose flour
- 4 ounces cooked ham, julienned
- 1/2 teaspoon salt
- 1/4 cup grated Parmesan cheese
- 1/8 teaspoon ground black pepper

DIRECTIONS

1. Preheat oven to 350 degrees F (175 degrees C).
2. Bring a large pot of lightly salted water to a boil. Add pasta and cook for 8 to 10 minutes or until al dente; drain.
3. In a large saucepan over medium heat, melt butter. Saute garlic 30 seconds. Whisk in flour, salt and pepper. Cook and stir until smooth. Pour in milk, a little at a time, stirring constantly. Bring to a boil for 1 minute. Stir in mustard and Colby. Continue to cook, stirring occasionally, until cheese is melted. Remove from heat and stir in pasta and ham.
4. Pour into a 2 quart baking dish. Sprinkle with Parmesan.
5. Bake 20 to 25 minutes, until bubbly and golden.

MOM'S BAKED MACARONI AND CHEESE

Servings: 6 | Prep: 5m | Cooks: 40m | Total: 45m

NUTRITION FACTS

Calories: 674 | Carbohydrates: 65.5g | Fat: 30.9g | Protein: 32.3g | Cholesterol: 87mg

INGREDIENTS

- 1 (16 ounce) package macaroni
- 1 cup milk

- 1 (10.75 ounce) can condensed Cheddar cheese soup
- 1 pound shredded Colby cheese

DIRECTIONS

1. Preheat oven to 350 degrees F (175 degrees C). Bring a large pot of lightly salted water to a boil. Add pasta and cook for 8 to 10 minutes or until al dente; drain.
2. Place macaroni in a 2 quart casserole dish. Stir in cheese soup and milk until well combined. Sprinkle with shredded Colby.
3. Bake 25 to 30 minutes, or until cheese is brown and bubbly.

BAKED MACARONI AND CHEESE

Servings: 5 | Prep: 10m | Cooks: 35m | Total: 45m

NUTRITION FACTS

Calories: 570 | Carbohydrates: 43.9g | Fat: 31.6g | Protein: 28.2g | Cholesterol: 95mg

INGREDIENTS

- 2 slices bacon
- 3 cups shredded Cheddar cheese
- 8 ounces penne pasta
- 2 tablespoons butter
- 1 onion, chopped
- 3 tablespoons all-purpose flour
- 1 clove garlic, minced
- 2 cups milk

DIRECTIONS

1. Preheat oven to 350 degrees F (175 degrees C). Watch Now
2. Place bacon in a large, deep skillet. Cook over medium high heat until evenly brown. Drain, crumble and set aside. Watch Now
3. In a large pot with boiling salted water cook pasta until al dente. Drain. Watch Now
4. In a medium skillet saute the chopped onion, and minced garlic. Take off heat and add chopped cooked bacon and set aside. Watch Now
5. To make the sauce, in a medium saucepan melt the butter or margarine over low heat. Once melted, add the flour and stir constantly for 2 minutes. Gradually add milk and continue stirring until thickened. Stir in 2 cups of the grated Cheddar cheese and stir until melted. Watch Now
6. Combine cooked pasta, sauteed vegetables and sauce. Pour into a 2 quart casserole dish. Add the last cup of grated Cheddar cheese to top of mixture. Watch Now
7. Bake uncovered in preheated oven until cheese on top is melted and brown, 15 to 20 minutes. Serve warm. Watch Now.

ALLIE'S DELICIOUS MACARONI AND CHEESE

Servings: 6 | Prep: 10m | Cooks: 50m | Total: 1h

NUTRITION FACTS

Calories: 612 | Carbohydrates: 43.3g | Fat: 34.1g | Protein: 32.1g | Cholesterol: 110mg

INGREDIENTS

- 1 (8 ounce) package elbow macaroni
- 1/4 pound cubed ham
- 5 tablespoons butter
- 5 ounces cubed Cheddar cheese
- 5 tablespoons all-purpose flour
- 5 ounces mozzarella cheese, cubed
- 1 quart warm milk (110 degrees F/45 degrees C)
- 5 ounces Monterey Jack cheese, cubed
- salt and pepper to taste
- paprika to taste
- 1 pinch cayenne pepper

DIRECTIONS

1. Preheat oven to 350 degrees F (175 degrees C). Grease a 9 x 13 baking dish. Bring a large pot of lightly salted water to a boil. Add pasta and cook for 8 to 10 minutes or until al dente; drain.
2. In medium saucepan, melt butter and stir in flour to make a roux. Cook 1 to 2 minutes, stirring constantly, then whisk in warm milk a little at a time to make a white sauce. Bring to a boil, then reduce heat and simmer. Mix in salt, pepper, and cayenne, and stir frequently until sauce thickens.
3. Remove pan from heat and stir in cheddar, mozzarella, jack and ham. Combine pasta with sauce and stir well. Pour into baking dish. Use paprika to make a decorative pattern on top. Bake 45 to 60 minutes, or until top is the desired crispiness. Let rest 20 minutes before serving.

CLASSIC MACARONI AND CHEESE

Servings: 6 | Prep: 10m | Cooks: 1h | Total: 1h10m

NUTRITION FACTS

Calories: 701 | Carbohydrates: 64.9g | Fat: 33.5g | Protein: 34g | Cholesterol: 103mg

INGREDIENTS

- 1 (16 ounce) package macaroni

- salt and pepper to taste
- 1 pound sharp Cheddar cheese, sliced
- 1 (12 fluid ounce) can evaporated milk
- 1 tablespoon butter

DIRECTIONS

1. Preheat oven to 375 degrees F (190 degrees C). Bring a large pot of lightly salted water to a boil. Add pasta and cook for 8 to 10 minutes or until al dente; drain.
2. Grease a 2 quart casserole dish. Place a quarter of the macaroni in the bottom, followed by an even layer of one-quarter of the cheese slices. Dot with butter and season with salt and pepper. Repeat layering three times. Pour evaporated milk evenly over the top of all.
3. Bake, uncovered, for one hour, or until top is golden brown.

ALL DAY MACARONI AND CHEESE
Servings: 6 | Prep: 15m | Cooks: 6h10m | Total: 6h25m

NUTRITION FACTS

Calories: 648 | Carbohydrates: 38.5g | Fat: 38.7g | Protein: 36.2g | Cholesterol: 182mg

INGREDIENTS

- 8 ounces elbow macaroni
- 2 eggs
- 4 cups shredded sharp Cheddar cheese
- 1 teaspoon salt
- 1 (12 fluid ounce) can evaporated milk
- 1/2 teaspoon ground black pepper
- 1 1/2 cups milk

DIRECTIONS

1. In a large pot, cook the macaroni in boiling water 10 minutes, or until al dente, and drain.
2. In a large bowl, mix the cooked macaroni, 3 cups of the sharp Cheddar cheese, evaporated milk, milk, eggs, salt, and pepper. Transfer to a slow cooker that has been coated with non-stick cooking spray. Sprinkle with the remaining 1 cup of shredded sharp Cheddar cheese.
3. Cover, and cook on Low for 5 to 6 hours, or until the mixture is firm and golden around the edges. Do not remove the cover or stir the mixture until the mixture has finished cooking. Serve warm.

BAKED MACARONI AND CHEESE
Servings: 10 | Prep: 15m | Cooks: 30m | Total: 45m

Calories: 353 | Carbohydrates: 37.4g | Fat: 15.7g | Protein: 15.1g | Cholesterol: 75mg

INGREDIENTS

- 1 (16 ounce) package elbow macaroni
- 1/2 teaspoon black pepper
- 1/2 cup evaporated milk
- 1 1/2 cups shredded Cheddar cheese
- 2 eggs
- 1/2 cup grated Parmesan cheese
- 1 (8 ounce) container sour cream
- 1 tablespoon butter
- 1 teaspoon seasoning salt

DIRECTIONS

1. Preheat oven to 350 degrees F (175 degrees C).
2. Bring a large pot of lightly salted water to a boil. Add pasta and cook for 8 to 10 minutes or until al dente; drain and rinse with cold water.
3. In a bowl mix milk, eggs, sour cream, seasoning salt, and pepper. Layer macaroni, cheddar cheese, and milk mixture until pan is full. Sprinkle Parmesan cheese and pour melted butter on top.
4. Bake in a preheated oven for 20 to 30 minutes or until milk mixture is done.

CHEESE'S BAKED MACARONI AND CHEESE
Servings: 8 | Prep: 20m | Cooks: 45m | Total: 1h20m | Additional: 15m

NUTRITION FACTS

Calories: 600 | Carbohydrates: 39.2g | Fat: 38.3g | Protein: 24.1g | Cholesterol: 101mg

INGREDIENTS

- 1 (16 ounce) package fully cooked kielbasa sausage, cut into 1/2-inch pieces
- 2 cups milk
- 1 (8 ounce) package elbow macaroni
- 1 (10 ounce) package sharp Cheddar cheese, cubed
- 1/3 cup butter
- salt and ground black pepper to taste
- 1 small onion, chopped
- 1 cup dry bread crumbs, or more as needed
- 3 tablespoons all-purpose flour

DIRECTIONS

1. Cook and stir the cut-up kielbasa in a large skillet over medium heat for 6 to 8 minutes, until heated through and beginning to brown. Remove the sausage from the skillet, and set aside.
2. Fill a pan with lightly salted water, bring to a boil over medium-high heat, stir in the macaroni, and return to a boil. Cook, stirring occasionally, until the pasta has cooked through but is still firm to the bite, about 8 minutes. Drain well.
3. Preheat an oven to 350 degrees F (175 degrees C). Grease a 9x13 inch baking dish.
4. Melt the butter in the skillet over medium-low heat, and cook and stir the chopped onion for about 5 minutes, until translucent. Whisk in the flour, stirring constantly to avoid lumps. Cook and stir the butter, onion and flour for 2 to 3 minutes to make a roux, and remove from the heat. Whisk in the milk a little at a time, stirring constantly, until all the milk has been incorporated, and return to low heat. Bring the sauce to a simmer, and cook over low heat for about 2 minutes, stirring constantly, to finish cooking the flour. Whisk in the Cheddar cheese, a few cubes at a time, until all the cheese has been incorporated and the sauce is hot and smooth.
5. Pour the macaroni into the cheese sauce, and stir to combine. Stir in the cooked kielbasa, salt, and pepper.
6. Spoon the macaroni mixture into the prepared baking dish, and sprinkle the bread crumbs over the top. Bake for about 20 minutes in the preheated oven, until the crumbs are brown and the casserole is bubbling. Let stand for 15 minutes after baking, to set before serving.

SLOW COOKER MAC AND CHEESE
Servings: 12 | Prep: 15m | Cooks: 3h10m | Total: 3h25m

NUTRITION FACTS

Calories: 432 | Carbohydrates: 33.9g | Fat: 24.7g | Protein: 17.8g | Cholesterol: 99mg

INGREDIENTS

- 1 (16 ounce) package elbow macaroni
- 2 eggs, well beaten
- 1/2 cup butter
- 2 cups whole milk
- salt and ground black pepper to taste
- 1 (10.75 ounce) can condensed Cheddar cheese soup (such as Campbell's)
- 1 (16 ounce) package shredded Cheddar cheese, divided
- 1 pinch paprika, or as desired (optional)
- 1 (5 ounce) can evaporated milk

DIRECTIONS

1. Bring a large pot of lightly salted water to a boil. Cook elbow macaroni in the boiling water, stirring occasionally until cooked through but firm to the bite, 8 minutes. Drain and transfer pasta to slow cooker.
2. Add butter to pasta and stir until melted; season with salt and pepper. Sprinkle about 1/2 the Cheddar cheese over pasta and stir.
3. Whisk evaporated milk and eggs together in a bowl until smooth; stir into pasta mixture.
4. Whisk milk and Cheddar cheese soup together in a bowl until smooth; stir into pasta mixture. Sprinkle remaining cheese over pasta mixture; garnish with paprika.
5. Cook on Low for 3 hours.

BAKED MAC AND CHEESE FOR ONE

Servings: 1 | Prep: 10m | Cooks: 20m | Total: 30m

NUTRITION FACTS

Calories: 469 | Carbohydrates: 30g | Fat: 30g | Protein: 19.8g | Cholesterol: 89mg

INGREDIENTS

- 3 tablespoons uncooked macaroni pasta
- 1/3 cup shredded Cheddar cheese
- 1 tablespoon butter
- 1/8 teaspoon ground mustard
- 1 tablespoon all-purpose flour
- 1 dash Worcestershire sauce
- 1/4 teaspoon salt
- 1 dash hot sauce
- 1 pinch pepper
- 1 teaspoon bread crumbs
- 1/8 teaspoon onion powder
- 1 tablespoon shredded Cheddar cheese
- 1/2 cup milk

DIRECTIONS

1. Preheat an oven to 400 degrees F (200 degrees C). Grease an oven-proof soup crock or 1 cup baking dish.
2. Fill a small saucepan with water, and bring to a boil. Stir in the macaroni; boil until cooked but still firm to the bite, about 8 minutes. Drain well, and reserve.
3. In the same saucepan, melt the butter over medium-high heat. Stir in the flour, salt, pepper, onion powder, and milk; whisk until smooth. Cook, stirring, for 2 minutes. Reduce heat to low, and whisk in 1/3 cup cheese, mustard, Worcestershire sauce, and hot sauce. Stir in the cooked macaroni. Spoon

the macaroni and cheese into the prepared dish. Sprinkle with bread crumbs and 1 tablespoon cheddar cheese.

4. Bake, uncovered, until the cheese is melted and the macaroni is heated through, about 10 minutes.

EASY PLEASY MAC N CHEESY - US NAVY STYLE

Servings: 6 | Prep: 15m | Cooks: 50m | Total: 1h5m

NUTRITION FACTS

Calories: 447 | Carbohydrates: 43.2g | Fat: 22.4g | Protein: 18g | Cholesterol: 58mg

INGREDIENTS

- 8 ounces elbow macaroni
- 1/2 cup milk
- 8 ounces processed cheese (such as Velveeta), cubed
- salt and ground black pepper to taste
- 1 (10.75 ounce) can condensed Cheddar cheese soup
- 1/2 cup crushed saltine crackers
- 1 cup sour cream
- 2 tablespoons butter, melted
- 1/4 cup freshly shredded Parmesan cheese

DIRECTIONS

1. Preheat oven to 350 degrees F (175 degrees C). Grease an 8x8-inch baking dish.
2. Fill a large pot with lightly salted water and bring to a rolling boil over high heat. Once the water is boiling, stir in the macaroni, and return to a boil. Cook the pasta uncovered, stirring occasionally, until the pasta has cooked through, but is still firm to the bite, about 8 minutes. Drain well in a colander set in the sink. Transfer the macaroni to a large bowl, and stir in the processed cheese cubes, Cheddar cheese soup, sour cream, Parmesan cheese, milk, salt, and black pepper. Pour into the prepared baking dish. Mix the cracker crumbs with the butter, and sprinkle over the casserole. Cover the casserole with aluminum foil.
3. Bake in the preheated oven until bubbling, about 30 minutes; remove foil and bake until crumbs are golden brown, 5 to 10 more minutes.

CAFETERIA MACARONI AND CHEESE

Servings: 6 | Prep: 20m | Cooks: 30m | Total: 50m

NUTRITION FACTS

Calories: 544 | Carbohydrates: 39.4g | Fat: 31.4g | Protein: 25.4g | Cholesterol: 92mg

INGREDIENTS

- 8 ounces macaroni
- 1 1/2 tablespoons butter
- 1 1/2 cups milk
- 3 1/2 cups shredded Cheddar cheese, divided
- 1 1/2 teaspoons ground mustard
- 1/2 cup bread crumbs
- 1 teaspoon Worcestershire sauce
- 2 tablespoons butter, melted
- 3/4 teaspoon salt
- 1/2 teaspoon paprika
- 1 dash hot pepper sauce

DIRECTIONS

1. Preheat oven to 350 degrees F (175 degrees C). Grease a 2 quart casserole dish.
2. Bring a large pot of lightly salted water to a boil. Add macaroni and cook for 8 to 10 minutes or until al dente; drain.
3. Heat the milk in a small saucepan. Stir in mustard, Worcestershire sauce, salt, and hot sauce. Set aside.
4. Stir 1 1/2 tablespoons butter and 3 cups cheese into the drained macaroni. Pour the hot milk mixture over the cheese and macaroni. Transfer to prepared baking dish. Sprinkle remaining 1/2 cup cheddar on top. Combine the bread crumbs with the melted butter, and spread over the top. Sprinkle with paprika.
5. Bake in preheated oven for 30 minutes, and then place under the broiler for 1 to 2 minutes.

MAC AND CHEESE

Servings: 4 | Prep: 20m | Cooks: 45m | Total: 1h5m

NUTRITION FACTS

Calories: 650 | Carbohydrates: 58.6g | Fat: 32.3g | Protein: 30.4g | Cholesterol: 91mg

INGREDIENTS

- 8 ounces elbow macaroni
- 2 cups milk
- 2 tablespoons butter
- 1 cup shredded Cheddar cheese
- 1/4 cup all-purpose flour
- 8 ounces cubed processed cheese food

DIRECTIONS

1. In a large pot with boiling salted water cook elbow macaroni until al dente. Drain.
2. In a medium saucepan, over medium heat melt butter or margarine. Whisk flour and stir vigorously. Add milk and cook until thick and bubbly, about 5 to 7 minutes. Add cheeses and stir until completely melted.
3. In a large bowl mix together the drained pasta and cheese sauce mixture. Toss to coat evenly.
4. Pour into a greased 2 quart casserole dish. Bake in a preheated 350 degree F (175 degrees C) oven for 30 minutes. Let stand 10 minutes before serving.

SOUTHERN MACARONI AND CHEESE PIE

Servings: 8 | Prep: 15m | Cooks: 40m | Total: 55m

NUTRITION FACTS

Calories: 621 | Carbohydrates: 29.8g | Fat: 43.1g | Protein: 29g | Cholesterol: 197mg

INGREDIENTS

- cooking spray
- 3 eggs
- 2 cups uncooked elbow macaroni
- 1 teaspoon salt
- 1/2 cup butter
- 4 cups shredded Cheddar cheese
- 2 (12 ounce) cans evaporated milk
- 1 pinch paprika, or to taste (optional)
- 1 tablespoon ground black pepper

DIRECTIONS

1. Preheat the oven to 425 degrees F (220 degrees C).
2. Spray a 9x13-inch casserole dish with cooking spray.
3. Fill a large pot with lightly salted water and bring to a boil. Stir in the macaroni and return to a boil. Cook pasta uncovered, stirring occasionally, until it has cooked through but is still slightly firm, about 8 minutes; drain.
4. Slowly melt butter in a large pot over low heat. Stir in evaporated milk and black pepper; cook until heated through.
5. Whisk eggs in a bowl until smooth; whisk about 1/2 cup of the evaporated milk mixture into the eggs, 1 tablespoon at a time, until thoroughly incorporated. Whisk the egg mixture back into the saucepan with evaporated milk mixture. Continue to heat gently, whisking constantly, until the evaporated milk mixture almost comes to a simmer and the sauce thickens.
6. Gently mix salt and cooked macaroni into the sauce and stir to combine.
7. Spoon 1/4 of the macaroni mixture in a layer into the bottom of the prepared casserole dish and top with 1 cup shredded Cheddar cheese. Repeat layers three more times; top last cheese layer with paprika to taste.
8. Bake in the preheated oven until casserole is bubbling, about 20 minutes.

MACARONI AND CHEESE WITH CARAMELIZED ONIONS AND BACON

Servings: 8 | Prep: 20m | Cooks: 1h | Total: 1h20m

NUTRITION FACTS

Calories: 942 | Carbohydrates: 56.6g | Fat: 59.5g | Protein: 45.6g | Cholesterol: 197mg

INGREDIENTS

- 1 (16 ounce) package elbow macaroni
- 1/8 teaspoon brown sugar

- 1/4 cup butter
- 1/4 cup chopped fresh parsley
- 1/2 cup sour cream
- 1/4 cup panko bread crumbs
- 1 egg, beaten
- 2 tablespoons butter
- 2 tablespoons cream cheese, softened
- 5 tablespoons all-purpose flour
- 4 cups grated Asiago cheese
- 3 cups milk
- 4 cups grated Vermont Cheddar cheese
- 1/2 teaspoon ground mustard
- 4 slices bacon
- 1/2 teaspoon paprika
- 2 tablespoons butter
- 1/4 teaspoon salt
- 1 large onion, sliced thin
- 1/2 teaspoon pepper
- 4 cloves garlic, minced
- 1 tablespoon hot pepper sauce

DIRECTIONS

1. Bring a large pot of lightly salted water to a boil, add macaroni and cook for 8 minutes (noodles will still be slightly hard). Drain noodles and transfer to a large bowl with 1/4 cup of butter and toss to coat. Whisk together the sour cream, egg, and cream cheese; add to the pasta and mix well. Stir in 3 cups of grated Asiago and 3 cups of grated Cheddar cheese, reserving the remaining 2 cups of cheese for the topping.

2. Place the bacon in a large, deep skillet, and cook over medium-high heat, turning occasionally, until evenly browned, about 10 minutes. Drain the bacon slices on a paper towel-lined plate and chop into small pieces.

3. Preheat an oven to 400 degrees F (200 degrees C).

4. Stir 2 tablespoons butter, the onion, and garlic into the bacon drippings in the pan and cook and stir for 2 minutes. Reduce the heat to medium-low, and add the brown sugar. Cook, stirring occasionally, for 10 to 15 minutes until the onions are very soft and golden brown. Mix the cooked bacon, parsley, and panko breadcrumbs into the onions, transfer mixture to a small bowl and set aside.

5. Return the skillet to the heat and melt remaining 2 tablespoons butter over medium-low heat. Whisk in the flour, and stir until the mixture becomes paste-like and light golden brown, about 5 minutes. Gradually whisk the milk into the flour mixture and bring to a simmer over medium heat. Cook and stir until the mixture is smooth and thickened. Stir in the ground mustard, paprika, salt, pepper, and hot sauce. Remove sauce from heat and let cool for five minutes.

6. Pour the sauce over the macaroni mixture, stirring well. Transfer to a greased 9x13 inch pan and sprinkle with the remaining 2 cups of Cheddar cheese. Top cheese with the onion breadcrumb mixture.
7. Bake in preheated oven until bubbling, hot and golden brown on top, about 30 minutes.

HOME-STYLE MACARONI AND CHEESE

Servings: 6 | Prep: 20m | Cooks: 30m | Total: 50m

NUTRITION FACTS

Calories: 634 | Carbohydrates: 46.3g | Fat: 40.1g | Protein: 22.2g | Cholesterol: 118mg

INGREDIENTS

- 7 ounces elbow macaroni
- 1/2 teaspoon ground black pepper
- 1/4 cup butter
- salt to taste
- 3 tablespoons all-purpose flour
- 3 dashes hot sauce, or to taste
- 2 cups milk
- 2 cups shredded Cheddar cheese
- 1 (8 ounce) package cream cheese
- 1 cup dry bread crumbs
- 4 slices canned jalapeno peppers, chopped
- 2 tablespoons butter
- 2 teaspoons Dijon mustard
- 2 tablespoons chopped fresh parsley

DIRECTIONS

1. Preheat oven to 400 degrees F (200 degrees C).
2. Bring a large pot of lightly salted water to a boil. Cook elbow macaroni in the boiling water, stirring occasionally until cooked through but firm to the bite, 8 to 10 minutes. Drain.
3. Melt 1/4 cup butter in a 3-quart saucepan over medium heat. Stir flour into melted butter and cook until smooth and bubbling, about 1 minute. Mix milk, cream cheese, jalapeno peppers, Dijon mustard, black pepper, and salt into flour-butter mixture; cook, stirring occasionally, until sauce is thickened, about 5 minutes. Mix macaroni and Cheddar cheese into sauce; pour into a 2-quart casserole dish.
4. Mix bread crumbs, 2 tablespoons butter, and parsley together in a bowl; spread over macaroni and cheese.
5. Bake in the preheated oven until golden brown, 15 to 20 minutes.

SMOKY FOUR CHEESE MACARONI BAKE

Servings: 8 | Prep: 40m | Cooks: 55m | Total: 1h40m | Additional: 5m

NUTRITION FACTS

Calories: 638 | Carbohydrates: 45.9g | Fat: 37.7g | Protein: 28.7g | Cholesterol: 111mg

INGREDIENTS

- 1 (12 ounce) package macaroni
- 1 cup grated Parmesan cheese
- 1/4 cup butter
- 1 (8 ounce) package cream cheese, cubed
- 1/2 cup minced onion
- 1 cup shredded Swiss cheese
- 1 1/2 tablespoons minced garlic
- 2 cups shredded Monterey Jack cheese
- 1/4 cup all-purpose flour
- 1/3 cup shredded sharp Cheddar cheese
- 1/2 cup half-and-half cream
- salt and pepper to taste
- 1 1/2 cups milk
- 1/2 cup bread crumbs
- 1/2 teaspoon dry mustard powder
- 1/2 cup grated Parmesan cheese
- 1/2 teaspoon liquid smoke flavoring (optional)

DIRECTIONS

1. Preheat oven to 375 degrees F (190 degrees C). Lightly grease a 9x13 inch baking dish.
2. Bring a large pot of lightly salted water to a boil. Add pasta and cook for 8 to 10 minutes or until al dente; drain.
3. Meanwhile, melt the butter in a large saucepan over medium heat. Stir in the onion, and cook for 3 minutes until it begins to soften. Add the garlic, and continue cooking until the onion has softened and turned translucent, about 2 minutes more. Slowly stir in the flour, and cook, stirring constantly for 5 minutes.
4. Stir in the half-and-half and milk, and bring to a simmer. Reduce heat to medium-low and stir in mustard powder and liquid smoke; simmer for 10 minutes, stirring occasionally. Add 1 cup of Parmesan cheese, along with the cream cheese, Swiss, Monterey Jack, and Cheddar cheeses; stir until melted. Season to taste with salt and pepper, then stir in the drained macaroni noodles. Pour into the prepared baking dish. Sprinkle the remaining 1/2 cup of Parmesan cheese and breadcrumbs over the macaroni.
5. Bake in preheated oven until bubbly and brown, about 30 minutes. Remove from the oven and allow to stand 5 to 10 minutes before serving.

RESTAURANT STYLE MAC AND CHEESE

Servings: 4 | Prep: 15m | Cooks: 10m | Total: 25m

NUTRITION FACTS

Calories: 376 | Carbohydrates: 34g | Fat: 18.9g | Protein: 17.1g | Cholesterol: 59mg

INGREDIENTS

- 1 1/2 cups macaroni
- 2 tablespoons heavy cream
- 6 ounces processed cheese, shredded
- salt to taste
- 1/2 cup shredded Cheddar cheese

DIRECTIONS

1. Bring a large pot of lightly salted water to a boil. Add pasta and cook for 8 to 10 minutes or until al dente; drain.
2. Return drained pasta to the pot. Mix in processed cheese, Cheddar cheese, and cream. Stir until cheeses melt. Sprinkle with salt.

KICKED UP MAC AND CHEESE

Servings: 8 | Prep: 30m | Cooks: 40m | Total: 1h10m

NUTRITION FACTS

Calories: 352 | Carbohydrates: 19.6g | Fat: 23.3g | Protein: 16.4g | Cholesterol: 69mg

INGREDIENTS

- 1 1/2 cups rotelle pasta
- 3 teaspoons hot pepper sauce
- 4 tablespoons butter, divided
- 1 cup shredded pepperjack cheese
- 1/4 cup all-purpose flour
- 1 1/2 cups shredded sharp Cheddar cheese
- 3 cups whole milk
- 1/2 cup grated Parmesan cheese
- 1 teaspoon dry mustard
- 1/3 cup dry bread crumbs
- 3/4 teaspoon salt
- 2 teaspoons chili powder
- 1/2 teaspoon ground white pepper

DIRECTIONS

1. Preheat oven to 375 degrees F (190 degrees C).
2. Bring a large pot of lightly salted water to a boil. Add pasta and cook for 8 to 10 minutes or until al dente; drain.
3. In a large saucepan over medium heat, melt 2 tablespoons butter. Whisk in flour and cook, stirring, 1 minute. A little at a time, whisk in milk, mustard, salt, pepper and hot sauce. Bring to a gentle boil, stirring constantly. Boil 1 minute, then remove from heat and whisk in pepperjack, Cheddar and Parmesan until smooth. Stir in cooked pasta and pour into shallow 2 quart baking dish.
4. Melt remaining 2 tablespoons butter. Stir in bread crumbs and chili powder. Sprinkle over macaroni mixture.
5. Bake in preheated oven 30 minutes. Let stand 10 minutes before serving.

WISCONSIN FIVE-CHEESE BAKE

Servings: 12 | Prep: 10m | Cooks: 15m | Total: 25m

NUTRITION FACTS

Calories: 328 | Carbohydrates: 30.8g | Fat: 15.4g | Protein: 16g | Cholesterol: 46mg

INGREDIENTS

- 1 (16 ounce) package elbow macaroni
- 1/2 cup sour cream
- 1 cup shredded mozzarella cheese
- 1/2 cup heavy cream
- 1 cup shredded Swiss cheese
- 1 tablespoon chopped fresh parsley
- 1 cup grated Parmesan cheese
- 1/2 teaspoon dried Italian seasoning
- 1 cup shredded provolone cheese
- 1/2 teaspoon garlic salt
- 1/2 cup ricotta cheese

DIRECTIONS

1. Preheat the oven to 400 degrees F (200 degrees C). Lightly grease a 9x13 inch baking dish. Bring a large pot of lightly salted water to a boil. Add macaroni, and cook until tender, 6 to 8 minutes. Drain.
2. In a large bowl, toss together the mozzarella cheese, Swiss cheese, Parmesan cheese and Provolone cheese. Remove about 1/2 cup for topping and set aside. In a separate bowl, stir together the ricotta cheese, sour cream and heavy cream. Season with parsley, Italian seasoning and garlic salt.
3. Pour the ricotta cheese mixture and drained macaroni into the bowl with the cheeses and toss lightly. Do not mix too thoroughly, it's better left messy. Pour into the prepared baking dish. Sprinkle the reserved cheese over the top.

4. Bake in the preheated oven until cheese is melted, about 10 minutes, then turn the oven to broil. Broil for about 5 minutes to brown the top.

BUFFALO CHICKEN MAC AND CHEESE
Servings: 8 | Prep: 15m | Cooks: 20m | Total: 35m

NUTRITION FACTS

Calories: 781 | Carbohydrates: 51.7g | Fat: 41.9g | Protein: 47.3g | Cholesterol: 157mg

INGREDIENTS

- 1 (16 ounce) package elbow macaroni
- 1 pinch ground black pepper
- 1 rotisserie-roasted chicken
- 2 cups shredded Cheddar cheese
- 6 tablespoons butter
- 2 cups shredded Monterey Jack cheese
- 6 tablespoons all-purpose flour
- 1/2 cup hot sauce (such as Frank's Redhot), or more to taste
- 3 cups milk
- 1/2 cup crumbled gorgonzola cheese

DIRECTIONS

1. Bring a large pot of lightly salted water to a boil. Cook macaroni in the boiling water, stirring occasionally until tender yet firm to the bite, 8 minutes. Drain.
2. Cut wings and legs off rotisserie chicken. Skin and bone wings and legs; chop or shred dark meat into bite-size pieces.
3. Melt butter in a large Dutch oven over medium heat. Whisk in flour gradually until a thick paste forms. Cook until golden, about 1 minute. Pour in milk, whisking constantly, until thickened and bubbling, about 5 minutes. Continue to cook until sauce is smooth, about 1 minute more. Reduce heat and season sauce with black pepper.
4. Stir Cheddar and Monterey Jack cheese into the sauce until melted and combined. Stir in hot sauce, adjusting to reach desired level of spiciness. Add blue cheese, chicken, and macaroni; mix well to combine.

BEV'S MAC AND CHEESE
Servings: 4 | Prep: 20m | Cooks: 10m | Total: 30m

NUTRITION FACTS

Calories: 314 | Carbohydrates: 27.3g | Fat: 16.8g | Protein: 13.1g | Cholesterol: 50mg

INGREDIENTS

- 1 cup elbow macaroni
- salt and pepper to taste
- 1 cup milk
- 2 tablespoons butter
- 3 tablespoons all-purpose flour
- 1 cup shredded Cheddar cheese

DIRECTIONS

1. Bring a large pot of lightly salted water to a boil. Add pasta and cook for 8 to 10 minutes or until al dente; drain and reserve.
2. In a microwave-safe bowl, combine milk, flour and salt and pepper to taste; whisk or beat until smooth. Add butter and cheese; microwave on high for 5 minutes and whisk until smooth. Microwave for an additional 4 to 5 minutes and whisk or beat until smooth and no lumps remain.
3. Add cooked pasta to mixture; stir and serve.

FOUR CHEESE MACARONI AND CHEESE

Servings: 9 | Prep: 20m | Cooks: 20m | Total: 40m

NUTRITION FACTS

Calories: 260 | Carbohydrates: 11.9g | Fat: 16.2g | Protein: 16.5g | Cholesterol: 69mg

INGREDIENTS

- 1/2 (8 ounce) package elbow macaroni
- 1 cup shredded Colby-Monterey Jack cheese
- 1 cup shredded sharp Cheddar cheese
- 1 egg, beaten
- 1 cup shredded provolone cheese
- 1 cup milk
- 1 cup shredded mozzarella cheese

DIRECTIONS

1. Bring a large saucepan of lightly salted water to a boil. Place macaroni in the saucepan and cook for 8 to 10 minutes, or until al dente; drain.
2. Preheat oven to 350 degrees F (175 degrees C). Lightly grease an 8x8 inch baking dish.
3. Spread the Cheddar cheese over the bottom of the baking dish. Top with a thin layer of macaroni. Top macaroni with Provolone cheese, another layer of macaroni, a layer of mozzarella and a third layer of macaroni. Top with a layer of Colby-Monterey Jack cheese. Pour the egg over all, followed by the milk.
4. Bake in the preheated oven 20 minutes, or until bubbly and golden brown.

EASY MAC AND CHEESE MUFFINS
Servings: 12 | Prep: 15m | Cooks: 40m | Total: 55m

NUTRITION FACTS

Calories: 208 | Carbohydrates: 18g | Fat: 10g | Protein: 11.1g | Cholesterol: 44mg

INGREDIENTS

- 2 cups uncooked elbow macaroni
- 1 1/2 cups shredded mozzarella cheese
- 1 tablespoon butter
- 1/2 cup seasoned dry bread crumbs
- 1 egg, beaten
- 2 teaspoons olive oil
- 1 cup milk
- 1/2 teaspoon salt
- 1 1/2 cups shredded sharp Cheddar cheese

DIRECTIONS

1. Preheat the oven to 350 degrees F (175 degrees C). Grease a muffin tin with nonstick cooking spray. In a small bowl, stir together the bread crumbs, olive oil and salt; set aside.
2. Bring a large pot of lightly salted water to a boil. Add the macaroni and cook for about 8 minutes, it should still be a little bit firm. Remove from the heat, drain and return to the pan; stir in the butter and egg until pasta is evenly coated. Reserve 1/2 cup of sharp Cheddar cheese and stir the remaining Cheddar cheese, milk and mozzarella cheese into the pasta. Spoon into the prepared muffin tin. Sprinkle the reserved cheese and the bread crumb mixture over the tops.
3. Bake for 30 minutes in the preheated oven, or until the topping is nicely browned. Allow the muffins to cool for a few minutes before removing from the pan. This will allow the cheese to set and they will hold their muffin shape.

TASTY BAKED MAC N CHEESE

Servings: 12 | Prep: 30m | Cooks: 25m | Total: 55m

NUTRITION FACTS

Calories: 455 | Carbohydrates: 31.3g | Fat: 29.7g | Protein: 16g | Cholesterol: 98mg

INGREDIENTS

- 1 (16 ounce) package elbow macaroni
- 1 egg yolk
- 1/2 teaspoon salt
- 2 tablespoons all-purpose flour
- 3/4 cup butter, softened - divided
- 1/2 teaspoon salt
- 1 cup sour cream
- 1/2 teaspoon ground cayenne pepper
- 1 tablespoon cream cheese, softened
- 1 cup milk
- 1 (8 ounce) package shredded sharp Cheddar cheese
- 1 (8 ounce) package shredded mild Cheddar cheese

DIRECTIONS

1. Preheat oven to 375 degrees F (190 degrees C). Line a 9x13-inch baking dish with parchment paper.
2. Bring a large pot of water to a boil. Cook elbow macaroni in the boiling water, stirring occasionally until almost cooked through and firm to the bite, about 7 minutes. Drain and transfer to a large bowl. Sprinkle macaroni with 1/2 teaspoon salt and stir 1/2 cup butter into the pasta.
3. Mix 1/4 cup butter, sour cream, cream cheese, sharp Cheddar cheese, and egg yolk together in a bowl. Stir flour, 1/2 teaspoon salt, cayenne pepper, and milk into the sour cream mixture.
4. Spread 1/4 cup sour cream sauce over bottom of prepared baking dish. Stir remaining sour cream sauce into macaroni. Pour macaroni into baking dish atop sauce layer; sprinkle mild Cheddar cheese over the casserole
5. Bake in the preheated oven until heated through and cheese topping has melted, about 15 minutes.

VELVEET DOWN-HOME MACARONI AND CHEESE

Servings: 5 | Prep: 25m | Cooks: 20m | Total: 45m | Additional: 20m

NUTRITION FACTS

Calories: 497 | Carbohydrates: 46.7g | Fat: 25.9g | Protein: 18.6g | Cholesterol: 75mg

INGREDIENTS

- 1/4 cup butter, divided
- 2 cups elbow macaroni, cooked and drained
- 1/4 cup flour
- 1/2 cup KRAFT Shredded Cheddar Cheese
- 1 cup milk
- 6 RITZ Crackers, crushed
- 1/2 pound VELVEETA, cut into 1/2-inch cubes

DIRECTIONS

1. Heat oven to 350 degrees F.
2. Melt 3 Tbsp. butter in medium saucepan on medium heat. Whisk in flour; cook 2 min., stirring constantly. Gradually stir in milk. Bring to boil; cook and stir 3 to 5 min. or until thickened. Add VELVEETA; cook 3 min. or until melted, stirring frequently. Stir in macaroni.
3. Spoon into 2-qt. casserole sprayed with cooking spray; sprinkle with Cheddar. Melt remaining butter; toss with cracker crumbs. Sprinkle over casserole.
4. Bake 20 min. or until heated through.

FOUR CHEESE MACARONI CASSEROLE

Servings: 6 | Prep: 20m | Cooks: 40m | Total: 1h

NUTRITION FACTS

Calories: 511 | Carbohydrates: 47g | Fat: 22.8g | Protein: 29.7g | Cholesterol: 75mg

INGREDIENTS

- 3 cups uncooked macaroni
- salt and pepper to taste
- 1 (28 ounce) can whole peeled tomatoes, drained and chopped
- 1 1/2 cups grated Cheddar cheese
- 1 teaspoon Italian seasoning
- 1 1/2 cups shredded mozzarella cheese
- 1 teaspoon dried oregano
- 3/4 cup freshly grated Parmesan cheese
- 1 teaspoon basil
- 1/4 cup crumbled feta cheese

DIRECTIONS

1. Preheat oven to 350 degrees F (175 degrees C).
2. Bring a large pot of lightly salted water to boil over high heat. Add macaroni, and cook until al dente, about 8 to 10 minutes. Drain, and pour hot pasta into a casserole dish.
3. Meanwhile, in a large bowl, stir together tomatoes, italian seasoning, oregano, basil, salt, and pepper.

4. Stir into the hot pasta 1 cup of Cheddar, 1 cup of mozzarella, and 1/2 cup of Parmesan. Continue to stir until the cheeses have melted. Then stir in tomato and herb mixture. Sprinkle 1/2 cup Cheddar, 1/2 cup mozzarella, 1/4 cup Parmesan, and 1/4 cup feta over the top of the casserole.
5. Bake in preheated oven for 15 to 25 minutes.

GINNY'S CHEEZY MACARONI

Servings: 6 | Prep: 10m | Cooks: 1h | Total: 1h10m

NUTRITION FACTS

Calories: 459 | Carbohydrates: 43g | Fat: 21.1g | Protein: 23.6g | Cholesterol: 52mg

INGREDIENTS

- 3 tablespoons margarine
- 1 teaspoon black pepper
- 2 1/2 cups macaroni
- 1 (8 ounce) package Cheddar cheese, shredded
- 1 teaspoon salt
- 4 cups milk

DIRECTIONS

1. Preheat oven to 350 degrees F (175 degrees C).
2. Place margarine in 9x13 inch baking dish and put in oven to melt. When margarine is completely melted, pour in macaroni, salt and pepper. Stir until macaroni is coated with butter. Sprinkle cheese over macaroni and then pour milk over all. Do not stir and do not cover dish.
3. Bake in preheated oven for 60 minutes. Do not stir while baking.

CHIPOTLE MACARONI AND CHEESE

Servings: 10 | Prep: 20m | Cooks: 30m | Total: 50m

NUTRITION FACTS

Calories: 556 | Carbohydrates: 44.2g | Fat: 31.5g | Protein: 23.3g | Cholesterol: 98mg

INGREDIENTS

- 1 pound elbow macaroni, cooked according to package directions
- 1/2 teaspoon Spice Islands Fine Grind Black Pepper (optional)
- 1 quart half and half, divided
- 1/4 cup Argo OR Kingsford's Corn Starch
- 1 chipotle pepper from canned chipotles in adobo sauce, or more to taste

- 2 cups shredded Monterey Jack cheese
- 5 chicken bouillon cubes
- 2 cups shredded pepperjack chees
- 3 cloves fresh garlic, roughly chopped
- 1 cup shredded pepper jack cheese OR sprinkle with Spice Islands Paprika
- 1 tablespoon Spice Islands Onion Powder

DIRECTIONS

1. Preheat oven to 350 degrees F.
2. Blend 2 cups half and half, chipotle pepper(s), bouillon cubes and garlic in a blender or food processor until well blended. Pour into a large saucepan; add onion powder, black pepper, remaining 2 cups of half and half and corn starch. Stirring constantly, bring to a boil; boil and stir for 1 minute or until very thick. Remove from heat.
3. Gradually stir in cheeses until melted. Add cooked pasta and stir until blended. Pour mixture into a greased 3-quart casserole dish (or 13 x 9-inch pan) and sprinkle with desired topping.
4. Bake for 25 to 30 minutes or until browned and bubbly around edges.

OLD SCHOOL MAC N' CHEESE

Servings: 20 | Prep: 30m | Cooks: 45m | Total: 1h15m

NUTRITION FACTS

Calories: 507 | Carbohydrates: 40.2g | Fat: 30.1g | Protein: 21.5g | Cholesterol: 76mg

INGREDIENTS

- 1 3/4 pounds whole-wheat macaroni
- salt and ground black pepper to taste
- 3/4 cup butter
- 1 (8 ounce) package shredded Cheddar cheese, divided
- 3/4 cup all-purpose flour
- 3 (8 ounce) packages shredded American cheese
- 6 cups milk, divided
- 1 (8 ounce) bag potato chips (such as Lay's), crushed
- 1 tablespoon Worcestershire sauce
- 1 cup shredded Cheddar cheese
- 1 teaspoon mustard powder
- 1/3 cup grated Parmesan cheese
- 1 teaspoon onion powder
- butter-flavored cooking spray
- 1 teaspoon cayenne pepper

DIRECTIONS

1. Preheat oven to 375 degrees F (190 degrees C).
2. Bring a large pot of lightly salted water to a boil. Cook elbow macaroni in the boiling water, stirring occasionally until cooked through but firm to the bite, 8 minutes; drain.
3. Melt butter in a large pot over medium-low heat. Slowly add flour to butter, whisking constantly; cook until brown and the mixture no longer smells of flour, about 5 minutes. Pour 1 cup milk into the flour mixture, whisking continually until fully incorporated, about 45 seconds; repeat twice. Add remaining 3 cups milk to the mixture, whisking to incorporate. Stir Worcestershire sauce, mustard powder, onion powder, and cayenne pepper into the mixture; season with salt and black pepper.
4. Reduce heat to low. Cook sauce, whisking frequently, until it begins to thicken, about 10 minutes. Add about half the package of shredded Cheddar cheese; stir continually until the cheese melts completely. Repeat with remaining half package of Cheddar cheese and the American cheese, about 4 ounces at a time. Once cheese is entirely incorporated, remove sauce from heat.
5. Stir drained macaroni into the cheese sauce to coat. Divide macaroni between two 9x13-inch baking dishes.
6. Mix crushed potato chips, 1 cup shredded Cheddar cheese, and Parmesan cheese in a bowl. Top the macaroni with the potato chip mixture evenly. Spray the potato chip mixture with cooking spray.
7. Bake in preheated oven until the crust is golden brown and the sauce is bubbling, 35 to 45 minutes.

SHANNON'S SMOKY MACARONI AND CHEESE

Servings: 10 | Prep: 20m | Cooks: 45m | Total: 1h15m | Additional: 10m

NUTRITION FACTS

Calories: 651 | Carbohydrates: 50.7g | Fat: 35.1g | Protein: 32.4g | Cholesterol: 107mg

INGREDIENTS

- 1 (16 ounce) package elbow macaroni
- 1 1/2 cups shredded Swiss cheese
- 6 tablespoons butter
- 1 cup grated Parmesan cheese
- 1/2 cup all-purpose flour
- 1/2 cup grated Parmesan cheese
- 5 1/2 cups milk, divided
- 1/2 cup dry bread crumbs
- 2 1/2 cups shredded smoked Gouda cheese
- 1 teaspoon ground cayenne pepper
- 1 1/2 cups shredded Cheddar cheese
- olive oil

DIRECTIONS

1. Preheat oven to 350 degrees F (175 degrees C).
2. Fill a pot with lightly-salted water and bring to a boil. Stir the macaroni into the water and return to a boil. Cook and occasionally stir until the pasta has cooked through, but is still firm to the bite, about 8 minutes; drain.
3. Melt the butter in a large pot over medium heat. Add the flour to the melted butter and whisk continually for 1 to 2 minutes to make a roux. Whisk 2 cups of the milk into the roux until smooth and then add the remaining milk. Raise the heat to medium-high and continue cooking and stirring until thickened, but not boiling. Stir the Gouda, Cheddar, Swiss, and 1 cup Parmesan cheese into the mixture; once the cheeses have melted completely, fold the drained macaroni into the mixture to coat. Pour the macaroni mixture into a 9x13-inch baking dish.
4. Stir 1/2 cup Parmesan cheese, bread crumbs, and cayenne pepper together in a small bowl; sprinkle over the macaroni. Drizzle the olive oil over the bread crumbs.
5. Bake in the preheated oven until golden and bubbly, about 30 minutes. Allow to rest 10 minutes before cutting.

SLOW COOKER MACARONI AND CHEESE

Servings: 8 | Prep: 20m | Cooks: 4h | Total: 4h40m | Additional: 20m

NUTRITION FACTS

Calories: 463 | Carbohydrates: 28.8g | Fat: 28.1g | Protein: 23.6g | Cholesterol: 110mg

INGREDIENTS

- 2 cups evaporated milk
- 2 tablespoons butter
- 1/2 teaspoon paprika
- 3 1/2 cups cubed Cheddar cheese
- 1 teaspoon salt
- 1 (8 ounce) package macaroni
- 1 egg, beaten

DIRECTIONS

1. Combine in slow cooker: evaporated milk, paprika, salt, egg, butter and cheese; stir. Cook on high for 1 hour
2. Bring a large pot of lightly salted water to a boil. Add macaroni and cook for 8 to 10 minutes or until al dente; drain.
3. Stir cooked macaroni into cheese sauce, reduce temperature to low and cook for 3 to 5 hours.

MACARONI AND CHEESE SOUTHERN STYLE

Servings: 8 | Prep: 15m | Cooks: 50m | Total: 1h5m

NUTRITION FACTS

Calories: 380 | Carbohydrates: 21.7g | Fat: 26.1g | Protein: 15.5g | Cholesterol: 122mg

INGREDIENTS

- 1 (7.25 ounce) package macaroni and cheese mix
- salt and ground black pepper to taste
- 1 1/4 cups evaporated milk
- 8 ounces thinly sliced Cheddar cheese, divided
- 2 eggs
- 1/2 cup butter, diced - divided

DIRECTIONS

1. Preheat oven to 350 degrees F (175 degrees C). Grease a 2 1/2-quart casserole dish.
2. Set cheese packet from mix aside. Bring a pot of lightly salted water to a boil. Cook elbow macaroni in the boiling water, stirring occasionally, until cooked firm to the bite, 5 minutes. Drain and reserve pasta cooking water.
3. Whisk contents of reserved cheese packet with evaporated milk, eggs, salt, and pepper in a bowl. Layer half the cooked macaroni in the prepared casserole dish, followed by half the Cheddar cheese slices in a layer. Dot with half the butter. Repeat layers, using remaining half of cooked macaroni, remaining Cheddar cheese slices, and remaining butter. Pour evaporated milk mixture over casserole. If evaporated milk mixture does not reach to the top of the casserole, pour in enough pasta cooking water to cover.
4. Bake in the preheated oven until bubbling, about 45 minutes.

BLEU CHEESE MACARONI

Servings: 6 | Prep: 5m | Cooks: 20m | Total: 25m

NUTRITION FACTS

Calories: 433 | Carbohydrates: 36.5g | Fat: 24.9g | Protein: 15.7g | Cholesterol: 76mg

INGREDIENTS

- 2 cups uncooked elbow macaroni
- 3/4 cup heavy cream
- 2 tablespoons butter
- 1/3 cup all-purpose flour
- 1 teaspoon salt
- 1/2 cup plain yogurt
- 1/2 teaspoon black pepper
- 1 cup crumbled blue cheese

- 1/2 cup sliced green bell pepper
- 1/2 cup grated Parmesan cheese
- 1/2 cup sliced red bell pepper

DIRECTIONS

1. Bring a large pot of lightly salted water to a boil. Add macaroni and cook for 8 to 10 minutes or until al dente; drain.
2. Meanwhile, in a medium saucepan over medium heat combine butter, salt, pepper and bell peppers. Simmer until heated through. Stir in cream, flour, yogurt, bleu cheese and Parmesan cheese.
3. Stir cooked macaroni into cheese mixture and serve hot.

CHEESE AND HAMBURGER MACARONI
Servings: 4 | Prep: 10m | Cooks: 15m | Total: 25m

NUTRITION FACTS

Calories: 449 | Carbohydrates: 47.9g | Fat: 15.4g | Protein: 28.2g | Cholesterol: 61mg

INGREDIENTS

- 1/2 pound lean ground beef, or more to taste
- 2 cups water
- 1/2 small onion, minced
- 2 cups elbow macaroni
- 1 teaspoon garlic powder
- 8 ounces reduced-fat processed cheese food (such as Velveeta), cut into small pieces
- 1 teaspoon onion powder
- 2 tablespoons reduced-fat sour cream, or more to taste
- 1 pinch salt and ground black pepper to taste

DIRECTIONS

1. Heat a large skillet over medium-high heat. Cook and stir ground beef, onion, garlic powder, onion powder, salt, and black pepper in the hot skillet until browned and crumbly, 5 to 7 minutes; drain and discard grease.
2. Return skillet to burner over high heat. Add water; cover skillet and bring to a boil. Stir macaroni into the boiling water-ground beef mixture; cover and lower heat to medium. Cook, keeping covered, for 5 minutes. Stir, cover, and cook until macaroni is tender, about 5 more minutes.
3. Stir processed cheese food into ground beef-macaroni mixture until melted. Remove from heat; stir in sour cream.

GREAT MAC AND CHEESE

Servings: 6 | Prep: 15m | Cooks: 20m | Total: 35m

NUTRITION FACTS

Calories: 408 | Carbohydrates: 38.9g | Fat: 20.4g | Protein: 17g | Cholesterol: 60mg

INGREDIENTS

- 1/4 cup butter
- 8 ounces macaroni
- 1 cup chopped onion
- 3 cups milk
- 1 1/2 tablespoons all-purpose flour
- 1 1/2 cups shredded Cheddar cheese
- 1 teaspoon salt

DIRECTIONS

1. Heat the butter in a skillet over medium heat. Stir in the onion; cook and stir until the onion has softened and turned translucent, about 5 minutes. Stir in flour and salt and cook, stirring constantly, for 2 minutes more.
2. Add milk and macaroni to saucepan, and bring to a boil. Reduce heat and cover. Simmer for 15 minutes or until pasta is tender, stirring occasionally.
3. Mix in cheese, and stir until cheese melts.

MAC AND CHEESE HENWOOD STYLE

Servings: 6 | Prep: 15m | Cooks: 35m | Total: 50m

NUTRITION FACTS

Calories: 375 | Carbohydrates: 35.8g | Fat: 19.4g | Protein: 15.1g | Cholesterol: 34mg

INGREDIENTS

- 1/2 (16 ounce) package fusilli (spiral) pasta
- 1/4 cup blue cheese crumbles
- 1/4 cup margarine
- 1/4 cup cubed Cheddar cheese
- 1 tablespoon minced onion
- 1 teaspoon salt
- 1/4 cup all-purpose flour
- 1 pinch ground black pepper
- 2 cups milk

- 1/4 teaspoon dry mustard
- 4 ounces processed cheese food

DIRECTIONS

1. Fill a large pot with lightly salted water and bring to a rolling boil over high heat. Once the water is boiling, stir in the fusilli, and return to a boil. Cook the pasta uncovered, stirring occasionally, until the pasta has cooked through, but is still firm to the bite, about 12 minutes. Drain well in a colander set in the sink.
2. Preheat oven to 400 degrees F (200 degrees C). Lightly grease a casserole dish.
3. Melt the margarine in a large saucepan over medium heat; cook the onion in the melted margarine until translucent, about 5 minutes. Whisk the flour into the onion mixture; cook 1 minute more. Slowly pour the milk into the mixture while whisking until the milk is entirely incorporated. Add the cheese food, blue cheese, Cheddar cheese, salt, pepper, and mustard; cook and stir continually the cheese has melted and the mixture is thick; fold the pasta into the mixture. Pour the mixture into the prepared casserole dish.
4. Bake in the preheated oven until the top begins to brown, about 20 minutes.

VEGAN MAC AND NO CHEESE
Servings: 4 | Prep: 15m | Cooks: 45m | Total: 1h15m

NUTRITION FACTS

Calories: 648 | Carbohydrates: 61.6g | Fat: 39.2g | Protein: 16.5g | Cholesterol: 0mg

INGREDIENTS

- 1 (8 ounce) package uncooked elbow macaroni
- salt to taste
- 1 tablespoon vegetable oil
- 1/3 cup canola oil
- 1 medium onion, chopped
- 4 ounces roasted red peppers, drained
- 1 cup cashews
- 3 tablespoons nutritional yeast
- 1/3 cup lemon juice
- 1 teaspoon garlic powder
- 1 1/3 cups water
- 1 teaspoon onion powder

DIRECTIONS

1. Preheat oven to 350 degrees F (175 degrees C).

2. Bring a large pot of lightly salted water to a boil. Add macaroni, and cook for 8 to 10 minutes or until al dente; drain. Transfer to a medium baking dish.
3. Heat vegetable oil in a medium saucepan over medium heat. Stir in onion, and cook until tender and lightly browned. Gently mix with the macaroni.
4. In a blender or food processor, mix cashews, lemon juice, water, and salt. Gradually blend in canola oil, roasted red peppers, nutritional yeast, garlic powder, and onion powder. Blend until smooth. Thoroughly mix with the macaroni and onions.
5. Bake 45 minutes in the preheated oven, until lightly browned. Cool 10 to 15 minutes before serving.

WALTER'S CHICKEN AND MAC

Servings: 6 | Prep: 15m | Cooks: 1h | Total: 1h15m

NUTRITION FACTS

Calories: 424 | Carbohydrates: 33.2g | Fat: 18.7g | Protein: 29.5g | Cholesterol: 82mg

INGREDIENTS

- 2 cups macaroni
- 1 (10.75 ounce) can condensed cream of chicken soup
- 2 cups diced, cooked chicken meat
- 1 cup milk
- 2 cups shredded Cheddar cheese
- 1 (4.5 ounce) can sliced mushrooms

DIRECTIONS

1. Bring a large pot of lightly salted water to a boil. Add macaroni and cook for 8 minutes or until al dente; drain.
2. Preheat oven to 350 degrees F (175 degrees C).
3. In a large bowl combine cooked macaroni, chicken, cheddar cheese, soup, milk and mushrooms. Place mixture in a 9x13 inch baking dish.
4. Bake uncovered in preheated oven for 50 to 60 minutes; serve.

ULTIMATE MACARONI AND CHEESE

Servings: 15 | Prep: 15m | Cooks: 45m | Total: 1h

NUTRITION FACTS

Calories: 413 | Carbohydrates: 36.4g | Fat: 22.2g | Protein: 19.2g | Cholesterol: 65mg

INGREDIENTS

- 1 (16 ounce) package elbow macaroni
- 1 teaspoon salt

- 6 tablespoons butter
- 4 cups milk
- 6 tablespoons flour
- 6 cups shredded sharp Cheddar cheese
- 2 tablespoons McCormick Mustard, Ground
- 1 1/2 cups panko bread crumbs
- 1 1/2 teaspoons McCormic Black Pepper, Coarse Grind
- 1 teaspoon McCormick Paprika
- 1 teaspoon McCormick Garlic Powder

DIRECTIONS

1. Preheat oven to 400 degrees F. Cook macaroni in large saucepan as directed on package for al dente pasta. Rinse under cold water; drain well.
2. Melt butter in same saucepan on medium heat. Sprinkle with flour and seasonings. Cook and stir 2 minutes or until well blended. Gradually stir in milk until smooth. Stirring constantly, cook 3 minutes or until sauce starts to thicken. Stir in cheese until melted and smooth. Remove from heat. Add macaroni; toss gently to coat. Pour into greased 13x9-inch baking dish. Mix panko and paprika; sprinkle evenly over top.
3. Bake 25 to 30 minutes or until bubbly and golden brown on top. Let stand 5 minutes before serving.

BAKED MACARONI AND CHEESE WITH TOMATO

Servings: 6 | Prep: 30m | Cooks: 45m | Total: 1h15m

NUTRITION FACTS

Calories: 740 | Carbohydrates: 71.4g | Fat: 37.9g | Protein: 28.3g | Cholesterol: 104mg

INGREDIENTS

- 1 pound macaroni
- 3 cups shredded Cheddar cheese
- 1 (10.75 ounce) can condensed tomato soup
- 8 tablespoons butter, divided
- 1 1/4 cups milk
- 1/4 cup dry bread crumb

DIRECTIONS

1. Preheat oven to 350 degrees F (175 degrees C). Bring a large pot of lightly salted water to a boil. Pour in pasta and cook for 8 to 10 minutes or until al dente; drain.
2. In large bowl, combine macaroni, soup, milk, cheese and 6 tablespoons butter. Pour into 9x13 baking dish. Top with bread crumbs and dot with remaining butter. Bake for 45 minutes or until golden brown and bubbly.

DANNY'S MACARONI AND CHEESE

Servings: 6 | Prep: 10m | Cooks: 30m | Total: 40m

NUTRITION FACTS

Calories: 316 | Carbohydrates: 33.5g | Fat: 13.4g | Protein: 15.3g | Cholesterol: 39mg

INGREDIENTS

- 1 (8 ounce) package elbow macaroni
- 1 (14.5 ounce) can stewed tomatoes
- 1 (8 ounce) package shredded sharp Cheddar cheese

DIRECTIONS

1. Preheat oven to 350 degrees F (175 degrees C).
2. Bring a large pot of lightly salted water to a boil. Add macaroni and cook until almost done, about 8 minutes; drain.
3. Mix cooked macaroni with tomatoes and shredded cheese. Pour into a baking dish and bake in a preheated oven for 30 minutes.

SMOKED GOUDA MAC AND CHEESE

Servings: 8 | Prep: 30m | Cooks: 15m | Total: 45m

NUTRITION FACTS

Calorics: 328 | Carbohydrates: 46.2g | Fat: 10.3g | Protein: 13.8g | Cholesterol: 32mg

INGREDIENTS

- 1 (16 ounce) package seashell pasta
- 1/2 teaspoon salt
- 2 1/2 tablespoons butter
- 1/4 teaspoon ground white pepper
- 2 tablespoons all-purpose flour
- 4 ounces smoked Gouda cheese, shredded
- 2 1/2 cups milk

DIRECTIONS

1. Preheat oven to 375 degrees F (190 degrees C). Lightly grease a 10 inch casserole dish.
2. Bring a large pot of lightly salted water to a boil. Add pasta and cook for 8 to 10 minutes or until al dente; drain.

3. Melt butter in a small saucepan over medium heat. Stir in the flour and cook until a roux forms. Stir in the milk, salt and pepper; cook, stirring constantly, until sauce is smooth and thick and coats the back of a spoon. Remove from heat and stir in cheese.
4. Combine cooked pasta and cheese sauce; transfer to prepared dish.
5. Bake in preheated oven for 15 minutes, or until heated through.

CHEDDAR-BACON MAC AND CHEESE

Servings: 6 | Prep: 20m | Cooks: 20m | Total: 40m

NUTRITION FACTS

Calories: 385 | Carbohydrates: 30g | Fat: 21.8g | Protein: 16.5g | Cholesterol: 60mg

INGREDIENTS

- 1 3/4 cups elbow macaroni, uncooked
- 2 cups milk
- 3 tablespoons butter or margarine
- 2 cups KRAFT Shredded Sharp Cheddar Cheese, divided
- 2 tablespoons flour
- 3 slices OSCAR MAYER Center Cut Bacon, cooked, crumbled

DIRECTIONS

1. Heat oven to 350 degrees F.
2. Cook macaroni as directed on package. Meanwhile, melt butter in large saucepan on low heat. Stir in flour; cook 2 min. or until bubbly. Gradually stir in milk; cook on medium heat until mixture comes to boil, stirring constantly. Simmer on low heat 3 to 5 min. or until thickened. Add 1 1/2 cups cheese; cook and stir 5 min. or until melted.
3. Drain macaroni. Add to sauce with bacon; mix lightly. Spoon into 1 1/2 quart casserole; top with remaining cheese.
4. Bake 20 min. or until heated through.

LISA'S MACARONI AND CHEESE

Servings: 8 | Prep: 10m | Cooks: 1h10m | Total: 1h20m

NUTRITION FACTS

Calories: 859 | Carbohydrates: 91.8g | Fat: 34.2g | Protein: 44g | Cholesterol: 94mg

INGREDIENTS

- 2 pounds elbow macaroni
- salt to taste
- 10 ounces shredded Swiss cheese

- 1/8 teaspoon onion powder
- 10 ounces shredded mozzarella cheese
- 1 pinch garlic powder
- 10 ounces shredded Cheddar cheese
- 1/4 teaspoon dried parsley
- 1/2 cup milk
- 3 tablespoons margarine

DIRECTIONS

1. Preheat oven to 350 degrees F (175 degrees C). Grease a 9x13 inch baking dish.
2. Bring a large pot of lightly salted water to a boil. Add pasta and cook for 8 to 10 minutes or until al dente; drain.
3. In a large bowl, combine macaroni, Swiss, mozzarella and Cheddar and stir until cheeses melt. Stir in milk. Season to taste with salt, onion powder, garlic powder, and parsley. Spoon into prepared dish, and dot with margarine.
4. Bake in preheated oven 50 to 60 minutes, or until top is crunchy.

LAZY BAKED MACARONI AND CHEESE
Servings: 12 | Prep: 15m | Cooks: 45m | Total: 1h

NUTRITION FACTS

Calories: 420 | Carbohydrates: 36.4g | Fat: 21.2g | Protein: 20.4g | Cholesterol: 121mg

INGREDIENTS

- 1 pound uncooked macaroni
- 4 eggs
- 2 tablespoons butter, melted
- 2 teaspoons mustard powder
- 1 pound shredded American cheese
- 1 teaspoon salt
- 2 (12 fluid ounce) cans evaporated milk
- 1/2 teaspoon ground white pepper
- 2 cups water
- 1/4 teaspoon cayenne pepper

DIRECTIONS

1. Preheat the oven to 350 degrees F (175 degrees C).
2. In a shallow three-quart baking dish, toss uncooked macaroni and melted butter together, to coat the macaroni and the inside of the dish. Add cheese, and stir lightly to distribute. In a medium bowl,

whisk together the evaporated milk, water, eggs, mustard powder, salt, white pepper and cayenne pepper. Pour into the baking dish with the macaroni.

3. Bake uncovered for 45 minutes, or until the center is set. Remove from the oven, and let stand for 5 minutes before serving.

LOBSTER MAC AND CHEESE

Servings: 8 | Prep: 30m | Cooks: 1h | Total: 1h30m

NUTRITION FACTS

Calories: 913 | Carbohydrates: 55.4g | Fat: 49.2g | Protein: 60.9g | Cholesterol: 218mg

INGREDIENTS

- 1 (16 ounce) package elbow macaroni
- 5 tablespoons butter
- 1 (2 pound) lobster, split
- 5 tablespoons all-purpose flour
- 2 tablespoons butter
- 1 pound shredded Gruyere cheese
- 1 small onion, diced
- 3 cups shredded Cheddar cheese
- 1 clove garlic, minced
- 1 cup grated Romano cheese
- 1 shallot, chopped
- kosher salt and pepper to taste
- 10 black peppercorns
- 3 tablespoons panko bread crumbs
- 2 cups milk

DIRECTIONS

1. Fill a large pot with lightly salted water and bring to a rolling boil over high heat. Once the water is boiling, stir in the macaroni, and return to a boil. Cook the pasta uncovered, stirring occasionally, until the pasta has cooked through, but is still firm to the bite, about 8 minutes. Reserve about 2 cups of the hot pasta water, then drain the pasta in a colander set in the sink, and rinse with cold water to cool. Set aside.
2. Return the pasta water to the large pot, and place the lobster halves in the pot, cut-side up. Return the water to a boil, then reduce heat to medium-low, cover, and steam the lobster just until the meat firms and turns opaque, about 3 minutes. Remove the lobster and allow to cool for a few minutes, then remove the meat and cut into bite sized pieces. Reserve the shells.
3. Melt 2 tablespoons of butter in a saucepan over medium heat. Stir in the onion and cook until the onion has softened and turned translucent, about 5 minutes; scrape the onions into a small bowl and

set aside. Place the reserved lobster shells, garlic, shallots, peppercorns, and milk into the saucepan. Bring to a gentle simmer over medium heat, and cook for 20 minutes.

4. Preheat oven to 350 degrees F (175 degrees C).
5. Melt 5 tablespoons of butter in a saucepan over medium-low heat. Whisk in the flour, and stir until the mixture becomes paste-like and light golden brown, about 10 minutes. Strain the milk through a mesh sieve. Gradually whisk the milk into the flour mixture, and bring to a simmer over medium heat. Cook and stir until the mixture is thick and smooth, 10 to 15 minutes.
6. Stir the Gruyere, Cheddar, and Romano cheeses into the thickened milk mixture until melted and smooth. Season to taste with salt and pepper, then stir in the reserved lobster, onions, and macaroni. Pour the macaroni into a 4 quart casserole and smooth the top. Sprinkle evenly with the panko crumbs.
7. Bake in the preheated oven until the sauce is bubbly, and the top is golden brown, 8 to 12 minutes.

FRIED MAC AND CHEESE BALLS

Servings: 8 | Prep: 40m | Cooks: 30m | Total: 7h10m | Additional: 6h

NUTRITION FACTS

Calories: 543 | Carbohydrates: 42.1g | Fat: 32.3g | Protein: 20.4g | Cholesterol: 146mg

INGREDIENTS

- 1 (7.25 ounce) package macaroni and cheese mix
- 1/2 teaspoon chili powder
- 2 tablespoons butter
- 1/2teaspoon ground black pepper
- 1/4 cup milk
- 1/2teaspoon white sugar
- 1 cup shredded Cheddar cheese
- 1/4 teaspoon salt
- 3/4 cup pimento cheese spread
- 1 pinch cayenne pepper, or to taste
- 1 cup shredded Italian cheese blend
- 4 eggs
- 2 cups Italian seasoned bread crumbs
- 3 tablespoons milk
- 1/2teaspoon paprika
- 4 cups peanut oil for frying, or as needed

DIRECTIONS

1. Fill a pot with lightly salted water and bring to a rolling boil over high heat. Stir in the macaroni, and return to a boil. Cook, uncovered, stirring occasionally, until the macaroni is cooked through but still firm to the bite, about 7 minutes. Drain. Stir in the 2 tablespoons butter, the 1/4 cup milk, and the cheese packet from the package.

2. While the macaroni is still hot, stir in the Cheddar cheese, pimento cheese spread, and Italian cheese blend, and continue to stir until melted. Place the macaroni and cheese mixture in a container and refrigerate until firm, about 4 hours.
3. Line a baking sheet with parchment paper. Remove the macaroni mixture from the refrigerator, and, using a cookie scoop, scoop into balls. Place mac balls on the prepared baking sheet and freeze for at least 2 hours.
4. Heat oil in a deep fryer or large saucepan to 350 degrees F (175 degrees C)
5. Whisk the bread crumbs with the paprika, chili powder, black pepper, sugar, and cayenne in a shallow dish; set aside. Beat the eggs with the 3 tablespoons milk in a small bowl. Remove the mac balls from the freezer, coat in the egg wash, and then dredge in breading.
6. Fry the mac balls in small batches until golden brown, 3 to 5 minutes. Drain briefly on a paper towel-lined plate; serve hot.

EASY WEEKNIGHT BACON MAC 'N CHEESE

Servings: 4 | Prep: 10m | Cooks: 5m | Total: 15m | Additional: 5m

NUTRITION FACTS

Calories: 467 | Carbohydrates: 30.2g | Fat: 26.8g | Protein: 27.9g | Cholesterol: 73mg

INGREDIENTS

- 2 cups uncooked penne pasta
- 1 (3 ounce) package cooked real bacon pieces or bits
- 1 (9 ounce) pouch Progress Recipe Starter creamy three cheese cooking sauce
- Progresso Italian style panko crispy bread crumbs
- 8 slices American cheese, diced

DIRECTIONS

1. Cook and drain pasta as directed on package; keep warm.
2. Meanwhile, in 2-quart saucepan, heat cooking sauce to boiling, stirring occasionally. Remove from heat; stir in cheese until melted. Reserve 1 tablespoon of the bacon; set aside. Stir in pasta and remaining bacon. If necessary, cook over medium heat until thoroughly heated, stirring occasionally. Mix reserved bacon with bread crumbs; sprinkle over pasta.

HOMESTYLE BEEF, MACARONI AND CHEESE

Servings: 4 | Prep: 10m | Cooks: 30m | Total: 40m

NUTRITION FACTS

Calories: 777 | Carbohydrates: 68.6g | Fat: 38.4g | Protein: 39.6g | Cholesterol: 124mg

INGREDIENTS

- 2 cups elbow macaroni
- 1 (11.5 ounce) can tomato juice
- 1 pound ground beef
- 1 (10 ounce) can whole kernel corn, drained
- 1 (10.25 ounce) can condensed tomato soup
- 1 1/2 cups shredded mozzarella cheese

DIRECTIONS

1. Bring a large pot of lightly salted water to a boil. Add pasta and cook for 8 to 10 minutes or until al dente; drain.
2. In a skillet over medium heat, brown the ground beef until no pink shows; drain excess fat. In the large pot, combine macaroni, beef, tomato soup, tomato juice and corn; heat through. Stir in cheese.

FANCY-BUT-EASY MAC N' CHEESE
Servings: 8 | Prep: 25m | Cooks: 55m | Total: 1h20m

NUTRITION FACTS

Calories: 505 | Carbohydrates: 56g | Fat: 23.1g | Protein: 20.4g | Cholesterol: 65mg

INGREDIENTS

- 1 small red onion, diced
- 1/4 cup brown sugar
- 1 (16 ounce) package small pasta shells
- 3 (11 ounce) cans condensed cream of Cheddar cheese soup
- salt and ground black pepper to taste
- 2/3 cup shredded Havarti cheese
- 1 pinch garlic salt
- 1/4 cup grated Parmesan cheese
- 1 tablespoon butter
- 1 1/3 cups shredded Cheddar cheese

DIRECTIONS

1. Preheat oven to 350 degrees F (175 degrees C).
2. Place the diced onion in a large pot of lightly-salted water; bring to a boil. Cook the pasta until al dente, 8 to 10 minutes; drain. Transfer the onion and pasta to a casserole dish; season with salt, pepper, and garlic salt. Stir the butter and brown sugar into the pasta mixture until the butter melts. Add the Cheddar cheese soup, Havarti cheese, Parmesan cheese and 1/3 cup of Cheddar cheese; stir well. Sprinkle remaining Cheddar cheese over top of the dish.
3. Bake in preheated oven about 45 minutes. Change oven setting to 'Broil' and cook until top is golden brown, about 4 minutes.

MACARONI AND CHEESE BAKE

Servings: 10 | Prep: 10m | Cooks: 25m | Total: 35m

NUTRITION FACTS

Calories: 316 | Carbohydrates: 45.4g | Fat: 6.6g | Protein: 17.1g | Cholesterol: 14mg

INGREDIENTS

- 2 (10.75 ounce) cans condensed cream of chicken soup
- 4 tomatoes, sliced
- 3/4 cup milk
- 12 slices processed sharp Cheddar cheese
- 1 pound elbow macaroni

DIRECTIONS

1. Bring a large pot of lightly salted water to a boil. Add pasta and cook for 8 to 10 minutes or until al dente; drain.
2. Preheat oven to 350 degrees F (175 degrees C). In a medium saucepan, heat soup and milk over medium heat until simmering. Remove from heat and stir in macaroni. Pour macaroni mixture into 9x13 baking dish. Place a layer of tomatoes, then a layer of cheese slices over macaroni. Repeat.
3. Bake for 25 minutes or until cheese is golden and bubbly.

BAKED BUFFALO CHICKEN MAC AND CHEESE

Servings: 8 | Prep: 15m | Cooks: 30m | Total: 45m

NUTRITION FACTS

Calories: 917 | Carbohydrates: 67.1g | Fat: 53.3g | Protein: 44.7g | Cholesterol: 180mg

INGREDIENTS

- cooking spray
- 1 (1 ounce) package ranch dressing mix
- 1 (16 ounce) package elbow macaroni
- 1 rotisserie chicken, meat removed and chopped
- 1 (16 ounce) container sour cream
- 2 cups shredded Cheddar cheese, divided
- 1 (8 ounce) package cream cheese, softened
- 1 cup panko bread crumbs
- 1 (12 fluid ounce) can evaporated milk
- 1/4 cup melted butter
- 1 (12 fluid ounce) bottle Buffalo wing sauce (such as Frank's)

DIRECTIONS

1. Preheat oven to 350 degrees F (175 degrees C). Spray a 9x13-inch baking dish with cooking spray.
2. Bring a large pot of lightly salted water to a boil. Cook elbow macaroni in the boiling water, stirring occasionally until cooked through but firm to the bite, 8 minutes. Drain.
3. Stir sour cream and cream cheese together in a bowl until smooth; add evaporated milk. Stir Buffalo wing sauce and ranch dressing into sour cream mixture; mix in shredded chicken, macaroni, and 1 1/2 cups Cheddar cheese. Pour macaroni mixture into prepared baking dish. Top with bread crumbs and remaining 1/2 cup Cheddar cheese; drizzle melted butter over the top.
4. Bake in the preheated oven until bubbling and golden, 20 to 30 minutes.

ELSIE'S BAKED MAC AND CHEESE

Servings: 4 | Prep: 10m | Cooks: 40m | Total: 50m

NUTRITION FACTS

Calories: 623 | Carbohydrates: 49.2g | Fat: 36.3g | Protein: 26.1g | Cholesterol: 114mg

INGREDIENTS

- 1 1/2 cups Borden Triple Cheddar Natural Shreds
- 1/4 cup Borden Vitamin D Milk
- 1 cup Borden Colby Jack Natural Shreds
- 1 cup Borden Half & Half
- 2 cups uncooked elbow macaroni
- 1/4 teaspoon cayenne pepper, or to taste
- 2 tablespoons Borden Butter
- 1/2 teaspoon ground black pepper
- 2 tablespoons all-purpose flour
- Salt to taste

DIRECTIONS

1. Preheat oven to 350 degrees F. Spray the inside of a 1 1/2-quart casserole dish with non-stick cooking spray. Combine Cheddar and Colby Jack cheeses in a medium bowl and set aside.
2. Cook macaroni in boiling salted water according to package directions; drain well and set aside.
3. Meanwhile, melt butter in a medium saucepan over low heat. Blend in flour, stirring constantly, until smooth and bubbly. Gradually whisk in milk and half & half. Stir constantly, until mixture boils and thickens (about 2 to 3 minutes). Remove from heat and add cayenne and black peppers, and 2 cups of the reserved cheese mixture; stir until cheese is melted and sauce is smooth.
4. Stir cooked macaroni into the sauce and season to taste. Place in the prepared casserole dish. Top with remaining 1/2 cup of cheese and dot with additional butter, if desired. Bake 25 to 30 minutes or until heated through and lightly browned.

BUTTERNUT SQUASH MAC AND CHEESE

Servings: 10 | Prep: 15m | Cooks: 1h5m | Total: 1h20m

NUTRITION FACTS

Calories: 414 | Carbohydrates: 51.9g | Fat: 15.6g | Protein: 17.7g | Cholesterol: 46mg

INGREDIENTS

- 1 butternut squash, halved lengthwise and seeded
- 2 cups milk
- 1 (16 ounce) package rotini pasta
- 6 ounces shredded white Cheddar cheese
- 2 tablespoons butter
- 6 ounces shredded Cheddar cheese
- 2 tablespoons all-purpose flour
- 1/4 cup seasoned dry bread crumbs, or as needed
- 1/2 teaspoon dry mustard

DIRECTIONS

1. Preheat oven to 400 degrees F (200 degrees C).
2. Place butternut squash, cut-side down, on a baking sheet.
3. Roast squash in the preheated oven until soft, 40 to 50 minutes. Remove squash flesh from skin and set aside. Reduce oven temperature to 375 degrees F (190 degrees C).
4. Bring a large pot of lightly salted water to a boil; cook the rotini at a boil until tender yet firm to the bite, about 8 minutes; drain.
5. Melt butter in a large saucepan over medium heat. Whisk flour and mustard into melted butter until smooth, about 1 minute. Gradually whisk milk into flour mixture until the mixture has the texture of heavy cream, 5 to 7 minutes. Remove from heat.
6. Stir butternut squash, white Cheddar cheese, and Cheddar cheese into milk mixture until cheese is melted. Stir rotini into cheese mixture. Pour cheese mixture into a 9x13-inch baking dish. Top with bread crumbs.
7. Bake in the preheated oven until bread crumbs are golden, about 10 minutes.

LOBSTER MAC AND CHEESE

Servings: 2 | Prep: 30m | Cooks: 30m | Total: 1h

NUTRITION FACTS

Calories: 975 | Carbohydrates: 61.8g | Fat: 53g | Protein: 63.3g | Cholesterol: 283mg

INGREDIENTS

- 2 teaspoons vegetable oil
- 1 pinch cayenne pepper, or to taste
- 2 lobster tails, split in half lengthwise and deveined
- 1/2 teaspoon salt, or to taste
- 2 tablespoons butter
- 3 drops Worcestershire sauce, or to taste
- 1 1/2 tablespoons all-purpose flour
- 4 ounces grated sharp white Cheddar cheese
- 1 1/2 cups cold milk
- 1 ounce grated Gruyere cheese
- 1/4 teaspoon paprika
- 1 cup elbow macaroni, or more to taste
- 1 pinch ground nutmeg
- 1/2 teaspoon fresh thyme leaves
- 3 tablespoons panko bread crumbs
- 2 tablespoons grated Parmesan cheese
- 1 tablespoon melted butter

DIRECTIONS

1. Preheat oven to 400 degrees F (200 degrees C). Butter 2 gratin dishes.
2. Heat oil in a skillet over high heat. Cook lobster tails in skillet until slightly golden and about halfway cooked-through, about 2 minutes per side. Transfer tails to a plate to rest. When cool enough to handle, remove lobster meat from shells and chop meat. Reserve shells.
3. Melt 2 tablespoons butter in the same skillet over medium heat. Whisk in flour; cook and stir until a paste forms and flour taste cooks off, 1 to 2 minutes. Add cold milk to flour mixture; whisk until completely incorporated. Bring to a simmer; reduce heat to low, and stir in paprika, nutmeg, and cayenne pepper. Cook, stirring occasionally, until thick, 3 to 4 minutes. Season sauce with salt.
4. Stir Cheddar cheese and Gruyere cheese into milk mixture until cheese is melted. Remove from heat and stir Worcestershire sauce into cheese sauce.
5. Bring a large pot of water with reserved lobster tails and a pinch of salt to a boil. Cook elbow macaroni in the boiling water, stirring occasionally, until cooked through but firm to the bite, about 8 minutes. Remove and discard lobster shells, drain pasta.
6. Stir macaroni into cheese sauce with thyme leaves. Divide macaroni mixture between the 2 prepared gratin dishes. Top macaroni with chopped lobster meat, poking meat down into macaroni mixture with a fork.
7. Stir bread crumbs and melted butter together in a bowl. Add Parmesan cheese and stir. Top each gratin dish with bread crumb mixture.
8. Bake in the preheated oven until golden and bubbly, 15 to 20 minutes.

CHIPOTLE MAC AND CHEESE

Servings: 12 | Prep: 30m | Cooks: 1h | Total: 1h30m

NUTRITION FACTS

Calories: 384 | Carbohydrates: 36.1g | Fat: 19.7g | Protein: 15g | Cholesterol: 55mg

INGREDIENTS

- 1 (16 ounce) package elbow macaroni
- 6 tablespoons all-purpose flour
- 3 cups whole milk
- 1 teaspoon paprika
- 1/2 cup butter
- salt and pepper to taste
- 1/2 cup minced onion
- 2 cups shredded extra-sharp Cheddar cheese
- 4 cloves garlic, minced
- 1 cup shredded Monterey Jack cheese
- 3 chipotle chiles in adobo sauce, finely chopped

DIRECTIONS

1. Fill a large pot with lightly salted water and bring to a rolling boil over high heat. Once the water is boiling, stir in the macaroni, and return to a boil. Cook the pasta uncovered, stirring occasionally, until the pasta has cooked through, but is still firm to the bite, about 8 minutes. Drain well in a colander set in the sink.
2. Preheat oven to 350 degrees F (175 degrees C).
3. Spray a 9x13 inch baking dish with cooking spray, and place the macaroni into the bottom of the dish. Heat milk in a saucepan until hot but not boiling.
4. Melt butter in a saucepan, and cook and stir the onion, garlic, and chipotle chiles until the onions are translucent, about 5 minutes. Whisk in flour, 1 tablespoon at a time, and let cook for about 3 minutes, whisking constantly to avoid burning. Whisk in the hot milk, 1/2 cup at a time, and stir in paprika, salt, and pepper. Bring the mixture to a simmer (do not boil), whisking constantly until thickened, about 2 minutes. Whisk in the cheeses, about 1/2 cup at a time, and stir until the cheeses have melted and the sauce is thick and smooth.
5. Pour the sauce over the macaroni in the baking dish, and stir gently to combine. Cover the dish with foil.
6. Bake covered until the dish is bubbling and the macaroni has absorbed some of the sauce, about 40 minutes. Uncover, and bake until golden brown on the edges, 10 to 15 more minutes.

CREAMY MUSHROOM MACARONI

Servings: 5 | Prep: 10m | Cooks: 30m | Total: 40m

Calories: 735 | Carbohydrates: 81.5g | Fat: 30.5g | Protein: 32.4g | Cholesterol: 66mg

INGREDIENTS

- 1 (16 ounce) package elbow macaroni
- 1 (10.75 ounce) can condensed cream of mushroom soup
- 1 tablespoon butter
- 1 pound processed cheese food, cubed
- 1/3 cup milk

DIRECTIONS

1. Bring a large pot of lightly salted water to a boil. Add pasta and cook for 8 to 10 minutes or until al dente; drain. Preheat oven to 350 degrees F (175 degrees C).
2. In medium saucepan over medium heat, combine butter, milk, mushroom soup and processed cheese. Stir until cheese is melted and mixture is smooth. Stir in cooked pasta. Pour into 2 quart baking dish and bake 20 minutes or until top is golden brown. Let stand 10 minutes and serve.

BAKED MACARONI AND CHEESE

Servings: 7 | Prep: 20m | Cooks: 40m | Total: 1h

NUTRITION FACTS

Calories: 584 | Carbohydrates: 64.5g | Fat: 24.3g | Protein: 27.9g | Cholesterol: 74mg

INGREDIENTS

- 1 pound macaroni
- 14 ounces extra sharp white Cheddar cheese, shredded, divided
- 1 (11 ounce) can condensed cream of Cheddar cheese soup
- 1 (14.5 ounce) can stewed tomatoes
- 1 1/2 cups milk
- 1/4 cup dry bread crumbs

DIRECTIONS

1. Bring a large pot of lightly salted water to a boil. Add pasta and cook for 8 to 10 minutes or until al dente; drain and reserve.
2. In a large saucepan over low heat, warm soup and add milk; stir. Add 1/4 of cheese to soup and remove mixture from heat when cheese is melted.
3. Preheat oven to 400 degrees F (200 degrees C).
4. Add macaroni and tomatoes to soup; stir and pour into a 9x13 inch baking dish. Cover with bread crumbs and remaining cheese.
5. Bake in preheated oven for 25 to 40 minutes or until the cheese is a golden brown; serve.

EASY ADD-IN MACARONI AND CHEESE

Servings: 6 | Prep: 20m | Cooks: 25m | Total: 45m

NUTRITION FACTS

Calories: 429 | Carbohydrates: 31.2g | Fat: 28.9g | Protein: 11.8g | Cholesterol: 28mg

INGREDIENTS

- 1 (7.25 ounce) package uncooked macaroni and cheese
- 3 tablespoons sour cream
- 1 (10.75 ounce) can condensed cream of mushroom soup
- 1 cup shredded Cheddar cheese
- 1/2 cup margarine
- 12 buttery round crackers

DIRECTIONS

1. Preheat oven to 350 degrees F (175 degrees C).
2. Cook the macaroni according to directions on the box. Remove from heat, drain, and add soup, 1/4 cup of the margarine, sour cream, shredded cheese, and the cheese packet from the box. Do not use milk as directed on the box.
3. Pour in a small casserole dish and top with crumbled crackers. Melt the remaining margarine and pour over the crackers. Bake in a preheated oven for 25 minutes.

MACARONI PIE

Servings: 8 | Prep: 30m | Cooks: 1h | Total: 1h30m

NUTRITION FACTS

Calories: 743 | Carbohydrates: 91.6g | Fat: 25g | Protein: 35.7g | Cholesterol: 136mg

INGREDIENTS

- 32 ounces elbow macaroni
- 4 cups shredded Cheddar cheese
- 3 eggs
- 1/4 teaspoon salt
- 3 cups milk

DIRECTIONS

1. Preheat oven to 350 degrees F (175 degrees C).
2. Bring a large pot of lightly salted water to a boil. Add macaroni and cook for 8 to 10 minutes or until al dente; drain.

3. Beat eggs and milk together. Pour half of the cooked macaroni into 9x13 inch baking dish. Cover macaroni with half of the cheese. Pour remaining macaroni into baking dish leaving a little room at the top. Cover with remaining cheese. Pour egg mixture over macaroni. Sprinkle with salt.
4. Bake in a preheated over for an hour or until a knife inserted comes out clean.

THREE CHEESE MACARONI WITH TOMATOES
Servings: 16 | Prep: 15m | Cooks: 40m | Total: 55m

NUTRITION FACTS

Calories: 432 | Carbohydrates: 52.5g | Fat: g | Protein: 19.8g | Cholesterol: 43mg

INGREDIENTS

- 2 pounds elbow macaroni
- 8 ounces white Cheddar cheese, cubed
- 8 ounces Colby-Jack cheese, cubed
- 2 (14 ounce) cans stewed tomatoes, undrained, crushed
- 8 ounces Cheddar cheese, cubed
- 1 cup dry bread crumbs

DIRECTIONS

1. Preheat oven to 350 degrees F (175 degrees C). Lightly grease a medium baking dish.
2. Bring a large pot of lightly salted water to a boil. Place macaroni in the pot, cook for 8 to 10 minutes, until al dente, and drain.
3. In the baking dish, mix the cooked macaroni, Colby-Jack cheese, Cheddar cheese, white Cheddar cheese, and tomatoes with juice. Sprinkle bread crumbs evenly over top.
4. Bake 30 minutes in the preheated oven, until bubbly and lightly brown.

TEX-MEX MACARONI AND CHEESE
Servings: 6 | Prep: 10m | Cooks: 20m | Total: 30m

NUTRITION FACTS

Calories: 384 | Carbohydrates: 27.1g | Fat: 21.1g | Protein: 19g | Cholesterol: 73mg

INGREDIENTS

- 1 pound lean ground beef
- 2 tablespoons butter, or as needed
- 1 (1.25 ounce) package taco seasoning mix
- 1/4 cup milk, or as needed
- 1 (7.3 ounce) package white Cheddar macaroni and cheese mix

DIRECTIONS

1. In a large skillet, brown beef and drain off excess fat. Add taco seasoning and water according to seasoning package directions and simmer for 10 minutes or until liquid is absorbed. Set aside.
2. Prepare macaroni and cheese according to package directions, adding butter or margarine and milk as indicated. Combine beef mixture and macaroni and cheese. Mix together and serve.

BAKED MAC AND CHEESE WITH SOUR CREAM AND COTTAGE CHEESE

Servings: 12 | Prep: 15m | Cooks: 50m | Total: 1h15m

NUTRITION FACTS

Calories: 415 | Carbohydrates: 29.6g | Fat: 23.2g | Protein: 21.5g | Cholesterol: 81mg

INGREDIENTS

- cooking spray
- 3/4 cup sour cream
- 1 (16 ounce) package elbow macaroni
- 3/4 cup cottage cheese
- 2 (8 ounce) packages mild Cheddar cheese, shredded, divided
- 1 egg
- 1 (8 ounce) package sharp Cheddar cheese, shredded
- salt and ground black pepper to taste

DIRECTIONS

1. Preheat oven to 350 degrees F (175 degrees C). Spray a 9x13-inch baking dish with cooking spray.
2. Bring a large pot of lightly salted water to a boil. Cook elbow macaroni in the boiling water, stirring occasionally, until cooked through but firm to the bite, 8 minutes; drain.
3. Reserve 1/2 cup shredded mild Cheddar cheese for later use
4. Mix mild Cheddar cheese, sharp Cheddar cheese, sour cream, cottage cheese, and egg together in a bowl; season with salt and pepper. Stir cooked macaroni into cheese mixture. Pour macaroni mixture evenly into the prepared baking dish; sprinkle with the reserved 1/2 cup Cheddar cheese.
5. Bake in the preheated oven until cheese is melted and bubbling, 40 minutes. Let cool for 10 minutes before serving.

TUNA MAC

Servings: 4 | Prep: 10m | Cooks: 40m | Total: 50m

NUTRITION FACTS

Calories: 447 | Carbohydrates: 56.3g | Fat: 15.2g | Protein: 21.1g | Cholesterol: 56.3mg

INGREDIENTS

- 6 cups water
- 1 (5 ounce) can tuna, drained and flaked
- 1 (7.25 ounce) package macaroni and cheese dinner mix
- 1 (4.5 ounce) can sliced mushrooms, drained
- 1/4 cup margarine, cut into pieces
- 1 cup bread crumbs
- 1/4 cup milk

DIRECTIONS

1. Preheat oven to 350 degrees F (175 degrees C).
2. Bring water to boil in a saucepan. Cook macaroni at a boil, stirring occasionally, until tender, 7 to 8 minutes; drain.
3. Return macaroni to the saucepan. Stir cheese sauce mixture from the packet, margarine, and milk into the macaroni until the margarine melts and the macaroni is evenly coated in sauce. Add tuna and mushrooms; stir. Pour macaroni mixture into a small casserole dish; top with bread crumbs.
4. Bake in preheated oven until hot, about 30 minutes.

SOUTHERN MACARONI AND CHEESE

Servings: 10 | Prep: 10m | Cooks: 50m | Total: 1h

NUTRITION FACTS

Calories: 477 | Carbohydrates: 38.9g | Fat: 24.3g | Protein: 25.1g | Cholesterol: 115mg

INGREDIENTS

- 1 (16 ounce) package uncooked elbow macaroni
- 2 cups shredded sharp Cheddar cheese
- 3 (8 ounce) containers cottage cheese
- 1/4 teaspoon cayenne pepper
- 1 (16 ounce) container sour cream
- 1 teaspoon paprika
- 3 eggs

DIRECTIONS

1. Preheat oven to 350 degrees F (175 degrees C). Grease a 9x13 inch baking dish.
2. Bring a large pot of lightly salted water to a boil. Add pasta and cook for 8 to 10 minutes or until al dente; drain.
3. In a large bowl combine cooked pasta, cottage cheese, sour cream, eggs, Cheddar cheese and cayenne pepper. Mix well and transfer to prepared dish. Sprinkle with paprika.
4. Cover loosely with aluminum foil and bake 40 minutes.

SPICY SLOW COOKER MAC-N-CHEESE

Servings: 8 | Prep: 10m | Cooks: 2h5m | Total: 2h15m

NUTRITION FACTS

Calories: 553 | Carbohydrates: 49.7g | Fat: 29.8g | Protein: 22.8g | Cholesterol: 74mg

INGREDIENTS

- 2 (11 ounce) cans condensed Cheddar cheese soup
- 1 cup sour cream
- 2 3/4 cups water
- 1 cup shredded Cheddar cheese
- 1 (16 ounce) package uncooked shell pasta
- 1 cup shredded mozzarella cheese
- 1/2 pound andouille sausage, sliced into rounds
- salt and black pepper to taste

DIRECTIONS

1. Stir the condensed soup and water together in a slow cooker until smooth. Add the shell pasta and andouille sausage. Set the slow cooker to High; cook 2 hours, stirring frequently to prevent sticking.
2. Once the pasta is tender, stir in the sour cream, Cheddar, and mozzarella until the cheeses melt. Season to taste with salt and pepper. Remove from heat, and allow to rest 15 minutes before serving.

SMOKY CHIPOTLE MAC AND CHEESE

Servings: 6 | Prep: 10m | Cooks: 35m | Total: 45m

NUTRITION FACTS

Calories: 758 | Carbohydrates: 74.1g | Fat: 36.5g | Protein: 34.7g | Cholesterol: 100mg

INGREDIENTS

- 1 (16 ounce) package elbow macaroni
- 1 chipotle chile in adobo sauce, finely chopped
- 1 (11 ounce) can condensed Cheddar cheese soup
- 1/2 cup panko bread crumbs
- 1 (12 ounce) can evaporated milk
- 1 tablespoon olive oil
- 1 pound shredded Colby cheese

DIRECTIONS

1. Preheat oven to 350 degrees F (175 degrees C). Grease a 2-quart casserole dish.
2. Bring a large pot of lightly salted water to a boil. Cook elbow macaroni in the boiling water, stirring occasionally until cooked through but firm to the bite, 8 minutes. Drain.
3. Stir soup, evaporated milk, Colby cheese, and chipotle chile into the cooked pasta until well combined. Spoon mixture into the prepared casserole dish.
4. Stir together panko bread crumbs and olive oil in a small bowl. Sprinkle bread crumb mixture over the top of casserole.
5. Bake in the preheated oven until the top is browned and the casserole is bubbling, 25 to 30 minutes.

SLOPPY JOE MAC AND CHEESE

Servings: 8 | Prep: 20m | Cooks: 1h | Total: 1h20m

NUTRITION FACTS

Calories: 832 | Carbohydrates: 61.3g | Fat: 46.5g | Protein: 41.1g | Cholesterol: 160mg

INGREDIENTS

- 1 (16 ounce) package elbow macaroni
- 1/4 cup all-purpose flour
- 1 1/2 pounds ground beef
- 1 teaspoon ground dry mustard
- 1 (14.5 ounce) can canned diced tomatoes
- 1 teaspoon salt
- 1 (6 ounce) can tomato paste
- 1/4 teaspoon ground black pepper
- 1 (1.3 ounce) envelope sloppy joe seasoning
- 3 cups half-and-half
- 1/4 cup butter
- 1 tablespoon Worcestershire sauce
- 1 small onion, minced
- 4 cups shredded sharp Cheddar cheese

DIRECTIONS

1. Bring a large pot of lightly salted water to a boil. Place macaroni in the pot, and cook for 8 to 10 minutes or until al dente; drain.
2. Preheat oven to 375 degrees F (190 degrees C). Lightly grease a large casserole dish.
3. Place the ground beef in a skillet over medium heat, and cook until evenly brown. Drain grease. Mix in diced tomatoes, tomato paste, and sloppy joe seasoning. Reduce heat to low, and simmer 10 minutes.
4. Melt the butter in a large pot over medium-high heat. Stir in the onion, and cook until tender. Mix in flour, mustard, salt, and pepper. In a bowl, mix the half and half and Worcestershire sauce. Gradually whisk half and half mixture into the pot. Bring to a boil, and cook 1 minute, until slightly thickened. Remove from heat. Mix in 3 cups of cheese. Stir cooked pasta into the pot, evenly coating

with the sauce. Transfer to the casserole dish. Layer with the beef mixture and top with remaining cheese.

5. Cover, and bake 30 minutes in the preheated oven. Remove cover, and continue baking 10 minutes, until bubbly.

MACARONI AND CHEESE

Servings: 6 | Prep: 15m | Cooks: 10m | Total: 35m

NUTRITION FACTS

Calories: 557 | Carbohydrates: 62.4g | Fat: 22.6g | Protein: 25.8g | Cholesterol: 67mg

INGREDIENTS

- 1 (16 ounce) package macaroni
- 1/8 teaspoon celery seed
- 2 1/2 cups shredded sharp Cheddar cheese
- salt to taste
- 1/2 cup plain yogurt
- ground black pepper to taste
- 1 tablespoon butter
- 1/4 tablespoon dried basil
- 1 (14.5 ounce) can stewed tomatoes

DIRECTIONS

1. In a large pot cook macaroni pasta in boiling salted water until al dente. Drain well.
2. In a large saucepan over medium heat, melt the grated Cheddar cheese, plain yogurt, butter or margarine, and tomatoes. Cook until smooth. Add salt, black pepper, basil to taste, celery seed and cooked pasta to saucepan. Stir until blended.
3. Turn off the heat and let sit for 10 minutes with lid on, stirring occasionally. Serve hot.

ISRAELI COUSCOUS AND CHEESE

Servings: 4 | Prep: 15m | Cooks: 10m | Total: 25m

NUTRITION FACTS

Calories: 359 | Carbohydrates: 31.4g | Fat: 20.7g | Protein: 11.5g | Cholesterol: 71mg

INGREDIENTS

- 2 teaspoons butter
- 1 pinch cayenne pepper, or more to taste
- 1 cup pearl (Israeli) couscous

- 3 ounces shredded sharp Cheddar cheese
- 2 cups chicken broth
- 1 tablespoon chopped fresh chives
- 1/2 cup heavy cream
- salt and freshly ground black pepper to taste
- 1/4 cup diced pimientos

DIRECTIONS

1. Melt butter in a large skillet over medium heat. Cook and stir couscous in the melted butter until slightly toasted, 2 to 3 minutes.
2. Pour in chicken broth and bring to a boil. Reduce heat to low and simmer until most of the stock is absorbed and the couscous have plumped, 6 to 7 minutes.
3. Stir heavy cream and pimientos into couscous; add cayenne pepper and cook until couscous is tender, 2 to 3 minutes. Add more broth if needed.
4. Remove from heat and stir in Cheddar cheese until melted; add chives and stir to combine. Season with salt, black pepper, and cayenne pepper to taste.

GRANDMOTHER'S MACARONI AND CHEESE

Servings: 4 | Prep: 5m | Cooks: 55m | Total: 1h

NUTRITION FACTS

Calories: 309 | Carbohydrates: 22.4g | Fat: 16.6g | Protein: 17.1g | Cholesterol: 94mg

INGREDIENTS

- 1 cup elbow macaroni
- 1 tablespoon prepared mustard (optional)
- 1 1/2 cups shredded Cheddar cheese
- 1 dash hot pepper sauce (such as Tabasco)
- 2/3 cup milk
- salt and ground black pepper to taste
- 1 egg, beaten

DIRECTIONS

1. Preheat oven to 375 degrees F (190 degrees C).
2. Bring a pot of lightly salted water to a boil. Cook elbow macaroni in the boiling water, stirring occasionally, until cooked through but firm to the bite, 8 minutes; drain.
3. Stir macaroni, Cheddar cheese, milk, egg, mustard, hot pepper sauce, salt, and pepper together in a bowl; pour into a baking dish.
4. Bake in the preheated oven until brown and thickened, about 45 minutes.

MAC AND 'SHEWS (VEGAN MAC AND CHEESE)

Servings: 4 | Prep: 5m | Cooks: 15m | Total: 20m

NUTRITION FACTS

Calories: 430 | Carbohydrates: 57.2g | Fat: 16.8g | Protein: 17.6g | Cholesterol: 0mg

INGREDIENTS

- 1 cup unroasted cashews
- 2 teaspoons onion powder
- 1 cup vegetable broth
- 1/2 teaspoon salt, or to taste
- 3 tablespoons nutritional yeast flakes
- black pepper to taste
- 3 tablespoons fresh lemon juice
- 8 ounces small shell pasta or macaroni
- 2 teaspoons white miso
- 1 1/2 cups arugula (optional)

DIRECTIONS

1. Blend cashews, broth, yeast, lemon juice, miso, and onion powder in a high-powered blender (such as a Vitamix(R)), scraping down sides with a spatula until completely smooth. Season with salt and pepper, keeping in mind that you want it just a little saltier than usual because it's going to be poured over other ingredients.
2. Meanwhile, bring a pot of salted water to a boil and cook pasta according to package directions.
3. Drain, return to pot, and stir in cashew sauce. Cook over low heat, stirring, until sauce thickens a bit and everything is deliciously creamy, about 3 minutes. Stir in arugula (if using) and add more salt, if needed. Serve immediately.

EASY GLUTEN-FREE MACARONI AND CHEESE

Servings: 8 | Prep: 15m | Cooks: 45m | Total: 1h

NUTRITION FACTS

Calories: 521 | Carbohydrates: 42.6g | Fat: 29.8g | Protein: 21g | Cholesterol: 86mg

INGREDIENTS

- 10 ounces gluten-free elbow pasta
- 1/4 cup cornstarch
- 1/4 cup butter
- 4 cups shredded Cheddar cheese, divided
- 1 1/4 teaspoons salt

- 2 gluten-free bread slices, toasted and broken into crumbs (optional)
- 3/4 teaspoon mustard powder
- 1 teaspoon butter, softened (optional)
- 4 cups milk
- 1/2 teaspoon paprika (optional)

DIRECTIONS

1. Preheat oven to 375 degrees F (190 degrees C). Grease a 9x13-inch baking dish.
2. Bring a large pot of lightly salted water to a boil. Cook elbow macaroni in the boiling water, stirring occasionally until cooked through but firm to the bite, 8 minutes. Drain.
3. Melt 1/4 cup butter in a saucepan over medium heat. Stir salt and mustard powder into melted butter and remove saucepan from heat.
4. Whisk milk and cornstarch together in a bowl until smooth; stir into butter mixture until well blended. Return saucepan to stove; cook milk mixture, stirring constantly, over medium heat until sauce is thickened, about 5 minutes. Remove saucepan from heat.
5. Stir 3 cups Cheddar cheese into sauce until heat from sauce melts cheese. Add pasta to cheese sauce and stir well; pour into the prepared baking dish.
6. Combine remaining 1 cup Cheddar cheese, gluten-free bread crumbs, 1 teaspoon butter, and paprika in a bowl; sprinkle over pasta mixture.
7. Bake in the preheated oven until top is crunchy, about 30 minutes.

BEST ONE POT CHEESE AND MACARONI

Servings: 6 | Prep: 15m | Cooks: 15m | Total: 30m

NUTRITION FACTS

Calories: 518 | Carbohydrates: 30.7g | Fat: 30.8g | Protein: 30.1g | Cholesterol: 93mg

INGREDIENTS

- 3 cups water
- 4 cups shredded Cheddar cheese
- 1/2 teaspoon salt
- 1 cup shredded Parmesan cheese
- 8 ounces seashell pasta
- 1/4 teaspoon ground black pepper
- 1 cup whole milk
- 1 teaspoon Dijon mustard (optional)

DIRECTIONS

1. Pour water and salt into a medium pot and bring to a rolling boil over high heat. Once the water is boiling, stir in the shell pasta, and return to a boil. Cook the pasta uncovered, stirring occasionally, until the water has cooked down a bit, about 5 minutes.
2. Stir in the milk, and continue boiling for another 5 minutes. Add the Cheddar, Parmesan, pepper, and mustard; stir until the cheese melts and the sauce is thick and creamy. The starch from the pasta thickens the sauce as the pasta cooks.

SPICY SMOKY MACARONI AND CHEESE WITH TURKEY BACON

Servings: 6 | Prep: 10m | Cooks: 35m | Total: 45m

NUTRITION FACTS

Calories: 747 | Carbohydrates: 64g | Fat: 41.4g | Protein: 32g | Cholesterol: 144mg

INGREDIENTS

- 1 (16 ounce) package uncooked shell pasta
- 1/2 cup fat free half-and-half
- 10 slices turkey bacon
- 1 teaspoon paprika
- 1 (1 pound) loaf processed cheese food (such as Velveeta), cubed
- 1/2 teaspoon cayenne pepper
- 3/4 cup heavy cream
- 3/8 teaspoon smoked paprika

DIRECTIONS

1. Bring a large pot with lightly salted water to a rolling boil. Stir in the shell pasta and return to a boil. Cook the pasta uncovered, stirring occasionally, until the pasta has cooked through, but is still firm to the bite, about 13 minutes. Drain well in a colander set in the sink.
2. While the pasta is cooking, place the turkey bacon strips between two paper towels on a microwave-safe plate. Cook in the microwave on High until the bacon is crispy, 4 to 6 minutes depending on the microwave. Allow the bacon to cool; crumble and set aside.
3. Once the pasta has cooked and is draining, combine the processed cheese, cream, and half-and-half in the pot that was used to cook the pasta. Cook and stir over medium heat until the cheese has melted and the sauce is bubbly. Remove from the heat; stir in the paprika, smoked paprika, cayenne pepper, and crumbled turkey bacon. Stir the cooked pasta into the sauce until evenly coated.

EASIEST HOMESTYLE MACARONI AND CHEESE
Servings: 20 | Prep: 20m | Cooks: 55m | Total: 1h25m | Additional: 10m

NUTRITION FACTS

Calories: 479 | Carbohydrates: 41.6g | Fat: 26.7g | Protein: 18.4g | Cholesterol: 59mg

INGREDIENTS

- cooking spray
- 1 (1 pound) package processed cheese (such as Velveeta), cubed
- 1 teaspoon salt
- 1 teaspoon ground black pepper
- 1 teaspoon vegetable oil
- 1 teaspoon paprika
- 2 (16 ounce) packages elbow macaroni
- 1 (16 ounce) package shredded sharp Cheddar cheese, divided
- 2 (15 ounce) jars Alfredo sauce
- dry bread crumbs

DIRECTIONS

1. Preheat oven to 350 degrees F (175 degrees C). Spray a 10 1/2x13 1/2-inch baking dish with cooking spray.
2. Bring a large pot of water to a boil; stir 1 teaspoon salt and vegetable oil into boiling water. Gradually stir macaroni into the boiling water and cook, stirring occasionally, until macaroni are tender but still slightly firm, about 10 minutes. Drain well and pour macaroni into prepared baking dish.
3. Pour Alfredo sauce into a 3-quart microwave-safe bowl and stir processed cheese into sauce; microwave on 60 percent power for 6 minutes. Stir sauce mixture and microwave for 5 more minutes on 60 percent power. Season with black pepper and paprika. Stir 1 cup shredded sharp Cheddar cheese into mixture until cheese has melted and sauce is thick and smooth.
4. Pour half the cheese sauce over macaroni and stir to coat; pour in remaining cheese mixture and stir again. Spread remaining shredded sharp Cheddar cheese over macaroni. Top casserole with bread crumbs.
5. Bake in the preheated oven until the casserole is bubbling, 45 minutes to 1 hour. Broil casserole under oven's broiler for 3 to 4 minutes if you like a browned top. Let macaroni and cheese stand for 10 minutes before serving.

CHEESE AND PASTA IN A POT
Servings: 8 | Prep: 15m | Cooks: 1h15m | Total: 1h30m

NUTRITION FACTS

Calories: 910 | Carbohydrates: 61g | Fat: 57.3g | Protein: 38.6g | Cholesterol: 154mg

INGREDIENTS

- 1 (16 ounce) package elbow macaroni
- 1 (14 ounce) can stewed tomatoes, undrained
- 1 1/2 pounds ground beef
- 1 (16 ounce) jar spaghetti sauce
- 1 tablespoon vegetable oil
- 1 (12 ounce) can mushroom stems and pieces, undrained
- 1 large onion, chopped
- 2 cups sour cream
- 2 cloves garlic, chopped
- 1 pound Colby-Monterey Jack cheese, shredded

DIRECTIONS

1. Preheat oven to 350 degrees F (175 degrees C). Bring a large pot of lightly salted water to a boil. Add pasta and cook for 8 to 10 minutes or until al dente; drain.
2. Place ground beef in a large, deep skillet. Cook over medium high heat until evenly brown and crumbled. Drain, excess fat, and set aside.
3. Heat oil in a large heavy skillet over medium heat. Saute onion until soft and translucent. Stir in garlic, and cook for 30 seconds. Add cooked beef, tomatoes, spaghetti sauce and mushrooms; bring to a boil. Reduce heat, and simmer 20 minutes.
4. In a 9x13 inch casserole dish, layer 1/2 of the pasta, 1/2 of the meat sauce, 1/2 of the sour cream and 1/2 of the shredded cheese. Repeat layers.
5. Cover, and bake in preheated oven for 45 minutes.

EASY GOULASH

Servings: 6 | Prep: 5m | Cooks: 25m | Total: 30m

NUTRITION FACTS

Calories: 495 | Carbohydrates: 64.6g | Fat: 14.2g | Protein: 26.1g | Cholesterol: 57mg

INGREDIENTS

- 1 (16 ounce) package elbow macaroni
- 1 (8 ounce) can tomato sauce
- 1 pound ground beef
- 1/2 cup shredded Cheddar cheese
- 1 (10.75 ounce) can tomato soup

DIRECTIONS

1. Preheat oven to 350 degrees F (175 degrees C).
2. Bring a large pot of lightly salted water to a boil. Cook elbow macaroni in the boiling water, stirring occasionally, until cooked through but firm to the bite, 8 minutes; drain macaroni and return to pot.

3. Heat a large skillet over medium-high heat. Cook and stir beef in the hot skillet until browned and crumbly, 5 to 7 minutes.
4. Stir tomato soup and tomato sauce into the beef; pour into pot with macaroni and stir. Transfer macaroni mixture to a 1.5-quart baking dish; top with Cheddar cheese.
5. Bake in preheated oven until the cheese is melted, 10 to 15 minutes.

LOBSTER-BACON MACARONI AND CHEESE

Servings: 6 | Prep: 15m | Cooks: 45m | Total: 1h

NUTRITION FACTS

Calories: 627 | Carbohydrates: 61g | Fat: 27.5g | Protein: 33.4g | Cholesterol: 109mg

INGREDIENTS

- 3 cups elbow macaroni
- 1 1/4 cups milk
- 6 slices thick-cut bacon
- 12 ounces cooked lobster tail meat, chopped
- 2 (10.75 ounce) cans condensed Cheddar cheese soup
- 2/3 cup panko bread crumbs
- 1 1/2 cups shredded Cheddar cheese
- 1/4 cup butter, melted

DIRECTIONS

1. Bring a large pot of lightly salted water to a boil. Cook elbow macaroni in the boiling water, stirring occasionally until cooked through but firm to the bite, 8 minutes. Drain.
2. Place bacon in a large skillet and cook over medium-high heat, turning occasionally, until evenly browned, about 10 minutes. Drain the bacon slices on paper towels and dice.
3. Preheat oven to 400 degrees F (200 degrees C).
4. Stir Cheddar cheese soup, Cheddar cheese, and milk together in a bowl. Stir pasta, bacon, and lobster into soup mixture. Pour pasta mixture into a 2 1/2-quart shallow baking dish.
5. Mix bread crumbs and butter together in a separate bowl; sprinkle over pasta mixture.
6. Bake in the preheated oven until bubbling and bread crumbs are lightly browned, 25 to 30 minutes.

FOUR-CHEESE TRUFFLED MACARONI AND CHEESE

Servings: 12 | Prep: 5m | Cooks: 45m | Total: 1h | Additional: 10m

NUTRITION FACTS

Calories: 565 | Carbohydrates: 42.8g | Fat: 31.2g | Protein: 29.1g | Cholesterol: 98mg

INGREDIENTS

- 1 (16 ounce) package cavatappi (corkscrew macaroni)
- 2 cups shredded sharp Cheddar cheese
- 6 tablespoons butter
- 1 1/2 cups shredded Swiss cheese
- 1/2 cup flour
- 1 1/2 cups grated Parmesan cheese, divided
- 5 1/2 cups milk, divided
- 1/2 cup dry bread crumbs
- 2 1/2 cups shredded smoked Gouda cheese
- 1 tablespoon truffle oil

DIRECTIONS

1. Preheat oven to 350 degrees F (175 degrees C). Butter a 9x13-inch baking dish.
2. Bring a large pot of lightly salted water to a boil. Cook cavatappi in boiling water, stirring occasionally, until cooked through but firm to the bite, about 8 minutes. Drain.
3. Melt butter in a large pot over medium-low heat. Whisk flour into butter until mixture has a thick, paste-like consistency, about 30 seconds. Slowly whisk 2 cups milk into butter-flour mixture until smooth. Stir in remaining milk, increase heat to medium high, and cook, whisking constantly, until mixture is thick and almost boiling, 5 to 10 minutes.
4. Stir Gouda cheese, Cheddar cheese, Swiss cheese, and 1 cup Parmesan cheese into milk mixture until cheese melts and cheese sauce is smooth. Fold cavatappi into cheese sauce; pour mixture into prepared baking dish.
5. Stir remaining Parmesan cheese and bread crumbs together in a small bowl. Sprinkle bread crumbs mixture over cavatappi mixture and drizzle truffle oil over the top.
6. Bake in the preheated oven until golden and bubbling, about 30 minutes. Cool for 10 minutes before serving.

SOUTH-OF-THE-BORDER MAC AND CHEESE

Servings: 4 | Prep: 10m | Cooks: 2h15m | Total: 2h25m

NUTRITION FACTS

Calories: 675 | Carbohydrates: 55.9g | Fat: 35.5g | Protein: 34.2g | Cholesterol: 110mg

INGREDIENTS

- 2 1/2 cups rotini pasta
- 1 (4 ounce) can diced green chile peppers, drained
- 1 (12 fluid ounce) can evaporated milk
- 2 teaspoons chili powder
- 8 ounces American cheese, cut into cubes
- 2 tomatoes, seeded and chopped

- 4 ounces shredded sharp Cheddar cheese
- 5 green onions, sliced

DIRECTIONS

1. Bring a large pot of lightly salted water to a boil. Cook the rotini at a boil until tender yet firm to the bite, about 8 minutes; drain.
2. Combine the rotini pasta, evaporated milk, American cheese, Cheddar cheese, canned green chiles, and chili powder in a slow cooker.
3. Cook on High, stirring twice, for 2 hours.
4. Stir tomatoes and green onions through the pasta mixture.
5. Continue cooking until the tomatoes are hot, 5 to 10 minutes.

CAULIFLOWER MAC-N-CHEESE

Servings: 4 | Prep: 10m | Cooks: 20m | Total: 30m

NUTRITION FACTS

Calories: 471 | Carbohydrates: 34.3g | Fat: 28.5g | Protein: 19.3g | Cholesterol: 78mg

INGREDIENTS

- 1 1/2 cups elbow macaroni
- 1/2 cup milk
- 1/2 cup cauliflower florets
- 1 1/2 cups shredded Cheddar cheese
- cooking spray
- 1/2 (8 ounce) package cream cheese
- 1 tablespoon olive oil
- 1/2 teaspoon salt
- 1 tablespoon all-purpose flour
- 1/8 teaspoon ground black pepper

DIRECTIONS

1. Bring a large pot of lightly salted water to a boil. Cook elbow macaroni in the boiling water, stirring occasionally until tender yet firm to the bite, 8 minutes. Drain.
2. Place a steamer insert into a saucepan and fill with water to just below the bottom of the steamer. Bring water to a boil. Add cauliflower, cover, and steam until tender, 5 to 6 minutes. Place cauliflower in a blender or food processor; blend until smooth.
3. Coat a large saucepan with non-stick cooking spray; place over medium heat. Add oil and flour; cook, stirring constantly, until a thick paste forms, 1 to 2 minutes. Add milk; cook and stir until mixture thickens, 3 to 4 minutes.

4. Mix cauliflower, Cheddar cheese, cream cheese, salt, and pepper into milk mixture; stir until sauce is smooth. Fold macaroni into sauce.

EASY NO-BOIL MACARONI AND CHEESE
Servings: 8 | Prep: 5m | Cooks: 1h | Total: 1h5m

NUTRITION FACTS

Calories: 474 | Carbohydrates: 31.2g | Fat: 27.6g | Protein: 24.7g | Cholesterol: 81mg

INGREDIENTS

- 2 cups uncooked elbow macaroni
- 4 tablespoons butter
- 1 pound shredded Cheddar cheese
- water to cover
- 1 (12 ounce) container small curd cottage cheese
- bread crumbs

DIRECTIONS

1. Preheat an oven to 350 degrees F (175 degrees C). Grease a deep 2 quart casserole dish.
2. Mix macaroni, cheese, and cottage cheese in a large bowl. Pour water into the dish just to cover noodles and cheese. Dot with butter. Sprinkle bread crumbs evenly over top.
3. Bake until macaroni is tender, and cheese is melted, about 1 hour.

BROCCOLI MAC AND CHEESE WITH BACON AND POTATO NUGGET TOPPING
Servings: 8 | Prep: 25m | Cooks: 1h5m | Total: 1h30m

NUTRITION FACTS

Calories: 543.7 | Carbohydrates: 53.8g | Fat: 0g | Protein: 29.7g | Cholesterol: 132.6mg

INGREDIENTS

- 1 (16 ounce) package elbow macaroni
- 2 cups milk
- 6 slices bacon
- 1 pinch salt and pepper to taste
- 2 teaspoons butter
- 1/4 teaspoon adobo seasoning
- 1 head broccoli, cut into florets

- 2 cups shredded Cheddar cheese, divided
- 1 small onion, chopped
- 2 cups shredded mozzarella cheese, divided
- 3 eggs
- 20 eaches frozen bite-size potato nuggets (such as Tater Tots)

DIRECTIONS

1. Fill a large pot with lightly salted water and bring to a rolling boil over high heat. Once the water is boiling, stir in the macaroni, and return to a boil. Cook the pasta uncovered, stirring occasionally, until the pasta has cooked through, but is still firm to the bite, about 8 minutes. Drain well in a colander set in the sink.
2. Preheat an oven to 350 degrees F (175 degrees C). Grease a 9x13 inch baking dish.
3. Place the bacon in a large, deep skillet, and cook over medium-high heat, turning occasionally, until evenly browned, about 10 minutes. Drain the bacon slices on a paper towel-lined plate. Crumble the bacon and set aside. Heat 1 teaspoon of butter in a skillet over medium heat. Stir in the broccoli and onion; cook and stir until the onion has softened and turned translucent, about 5 minutes.
4. Whisk together the eggs, the remaining 1 teaspoon of butter, and milk in a large bowl. Season with salt, pepper, and adobo seasoning. Stir in 1 cup of Cheddar cheese, 1 cup of mozzarella cheese, the broccoli mixture and half of the potato nuggets. Place macaroni into the baking dish and pour the cheese mixture over the pasta, mixing well. Top with the remaining 1 cup of Cheddar cheese, 1 cup of mozzarella, bacon, and potato nuggets. Cover with aluminum foil.
5. Bake in the preheated oven until golden brown, 40 to 45 minutes.

CANADIAN BACON MACARONI AND CHEESE

Servings: 2 | Prep: 15m | Cooks: 30m | Total: 45m

NUTRITION FACTS

Calories: 668 | Carbohydrates: 54.1g | Fat: 34.6g | Protein: 34.6g | Cholesterol: 85mg

INGREDIENTS

- 1 cup elbow macaroni
- 2 1/2 tablespoons all-purpose flour
- 6 slices Canadian-style bacon
- 1 cup canned tomatoes, half-drained
- 2 tablespoons margarine
- 1 cup shredded Cheddar cheese

DIRECTIONS

1. Bring a large pot of lightly salted water to a boil. Add macaroni and cook for 8 to 10 minutes or until al dente; drain.

2. While macaroni is boiling, fry bacon and place on paper towels to drain. Cut into bite size pieces.

3. Melt margarine in a large saucepan over medium low heat. Stir in flour, then tomatoes and wait for sauce to thicken, stirring occasionally. When thickness is to your liking, stir in cheese until it has melted. Stir in cooked macaroni and bacon and heat through. Serve hot.

SALMON MAC AND CHEESE

Servings: 8 | Prep: 20m | Cooks: 1h10m | Total: 1h45m

NUTRITION FACTS

Calories: 581 | Carbohydrates: 61g | Fat: 25.3g | Protein: 28.2g | Cholesterol: 115mg

INGREDIENTS

- 1 (16 ounce) package elbow macaroni
- 2 eggs, beaten
- 1/4 cup butter, softened
- 2 cups milk
- 1 tablespoon olive oil
- 1/2 cup vegetable stock
- 1 small onion, minced
- 1 (14.5 ounce) can peas and carrots, drained
- 1 (6 ounce) can salmon, drained and flaked
- 1 (8 ounce) can whole kernel corn, drained
- 1 tablespoon seafood seasoning (such as Old Bay)
- salt and pepper to taste
- 1 tablespoon red wine vinegar
- 3 slices day-old bread
- 2 1/2 cups shredded Cheddar cheese
- 3 tablespoons grated Parmesan cheese

DIRECTIONS

1. Preheat an oven to 350 degrees F (175 degrees C). Lightly grease a 9x13 inch baking dish.

2. Fill a large pot with lightly salted water and bring to a rolling boil over high heat. Once the water is boiling, stir in the macaroni, and return to a boil. Cook the pasta uncovered, stirring occasionally, until the pasta has cooked through, but is still firm to the bite, about 8 minutes. Drain well in a colander set in the sink. Transfer to a large bowl. Stir the softened butter into the macaroni.

3. Heat the olive oil in a skillet over medium heat; cook the onion in the oil until brown, about 5 minutes. Stir in the salmon and seafood seasoning and cook until warmed through, about 5 minutes more. Remove from heat and pour the red wine vinegar into the skillet and set aside to cool.

4. Mix together the Cheddar cheese, eggs, milk, and vegetable stock in a large mixing bowl. Add the salmon mixture, peas and carrots, and corn; mix. Stir in the macaroni. Season with salt and pepper. Spread into the bottom of the prepared baking dish.

5. Toast the bread and break into small pieces. Combine the toasted bread and Parmesan cheese in a food processor; blend until chopped into crumbs. Sprinkle over top of the dish.
6. Bake in the preheated oven until heated through, about 45 minutes. Allow to cool 15 to 20 minutes before serving.

HEALTHY CREAMY MAC AND CHEESE

Servings: 6 | Prep: 15m | Cooks: 45m | Total: 1h

NUTRITION FACTS

Calories: 335 | Carbohydrates: 42.8g | Fat: 11.5g | Protein: 18.3g | Cholesterol: 15mg

INGREDIENTS

- 1 head cauliflower, chopped
- 1 teaspoon mustard powder
- 1 (8 ounce) package elbow macaroni
- 1/2 teaspoon garlic powder
- 1 cup plain Greek yogurt
- 1/4 teaspoon cayenne pepper (optional)
- 1 cup low-sodium chicken broth
- 1/8 teaspoon ground nutmeg
- 2 tablespoons olive oil
- 1/4 cup grated Parmesan cheese
- 4 ounces reduced-fat Cheddar cheese, cubed
- 1/2 cup panko bread crumbs
- 3 tablespoons nutritional yeast flakes

DIRECTIONS

1. Preheat oven to 375 degrees F (190 degrees C).
2. Place a steamer insert into a saucepan and fill with water to just below the bottom of the steamer. Bring water to a boil. Add cauliflower, cover, and steam until tender, about 25 minutes.
3. Bring a large pot of lightly salted water to a boil. Cook elbow macaroni in the boiling water, stirring occasionally until cooked through but firm to the bite, 8 minutes. Drain and transfer to a 9x13-inch casserole dish.
4. Blend cauliflower, yogurt, chicken broth, and olive oil in a blender until smooth; pour cauliflower mixture into a saucepan over medium heat. Stir Cheddar cheese, nutritional yeast, mustard powder, garlic powder, cayenne pepper, and nutmeg into cauliflower mixture; cook and stir until cheese sauce is smooth, about 5 minutes. Pour cheese sauce over macaroni; toss to coat.
5. Bake in the preheated oven for 15 minutes. Mix Parmesan cheese and panko crumbs together in a bowl; sprinkle over macaroni. Bake until Parmesan cheese is melted, 3 to 5 minutes.

MAC AND CHEESE BAKE

Servings: 8 | Prep: 30m | Cooks: 50m | Total: 1h20m

NUTRITION FACTS

Calories: 883 | Carbohydrates: 73.7g | Fat: 47.9g | Protein: 38.5g | Cholesterol: 142mg

INGREDIENTS

- 20 ounces elbow macaroni
- 1 1/2 pounds shredded sharp Cheddar cheese
- 1/2 cup butter
- 3/4 cup bread crumbs
- 3/8 cup all-purpose flour
- 2 tablespoons melted butter
- 6 cups milk

DIRECTIONS

1. Preheat oven to 350 degrees F (175 degrees C). Grease a 9x13-inch baking dish
2. Bring a large pot of lightly salted water to a boil. Cook elbow macaroni in the boiling water, stirring occasionally, until cooked through but firm to the bite, 8 minutes; drain.
3. Melt 1/2 cup butter in a large pot over medium heat; stir flour into butter until smooth. Stream milk into the butter mixture while stirring; bring to a boil. Cook and stir until thickened, about 2 minutes.
4. Reduce heat to medium-low. Add Cheddar cheese in small batches, stirring each into the milk mixture and melting until adding the next. Add macaroni and stir to coat. Pour macaroni into prepared baking dish.
5. Stir bread crumbs and melted butter together in a small bowl; sprinkle over the macaroni.
6. Bake in preheated oven until the top is golden brown, 35 to 40 minutes.

MICROWAVE MACARONI AND CHEESE

Servings: 4 | Prep: 10m | Cooks: 10m | Total: 25m | Additional: 5m

NUTRITION FACTS

Calories: 659 | Carbohydrates: 54g | Fat: g | Protein: 31.2g | Cholesterol: 92mg

INGREDIENTS

- 8 ounces macaroni
- 3/4 cup milk
- 2 tablespoons butter
- salt to taste
- 2 1/2 tablespoons chopped onion

- ground black pepper to taste
- 16 ounces cubed processed cheese food

DIRECTIONS

1. In a large pot with boiling salted water cook the elbow macaroni until al dente. Drain and set aside.
2. In a 2-quart microwave-safe covered casserole dish, cook the onions and butter or margarine on high for 3 to 4 minutes.
3. Add the cooked and drained pasta, milk, and cubed cheese and stir. Cook for 11 to 12 minutes on high, stirring well after 4, 8, and 11 minutes. The mixture will still be runny at this stage. Add salt and pepper to taste.
4. Let stand for 5-8 minutes before serving. The sauce will thicken as it cools slightly.

AVOCADO MAC AND CHEESE

Servings: 6 | Prep: 15m | Cooks: 0m | Total: 15m

NUTRITION FACTS

Calories: 458 | Carbohydrates: 67.3g | Fat: 12.8g | Protein: 19.6g | Cholesterol: 6mg

INGREDIENTS

- 1 pound elbow macaroni
- 1 cup flat-leaf parsley leaves
- 1 1/2 cups skim milk
- 2 fully ripened Avocados from Mexico, halved, pitted, peeled and diced, divided
- 3 small garlic cloves
- 5 ounces reduced-fat sharp Cheddar cheese cut in 1/2-inch cubes
- 1/4 teaspoon ground nutmeg
- 1 tablespoon lime juice
- 1/4 teaspoon chili powder
- 1/2 cup chopped chives

DIRECTIONS

1. In large sauce pot, cook pasta in salted water according to package directions.
2. Meanwhile, in a small saucepan, combine milk, garlic, nutmeg and chili powder. Bring to a boil; reduce heat; simmer for 5 minutes. When pasta is almost cooked, place in blender the parsley leaves, 1 1/2 cups of the diced avocado, the cheese, lime juice and hot milk with garlic cloves; whirl until smooth. Drain pasta and return to sauce pot. Pour cheese sauce over pasta; toss to combine. Add chives and remaining 1/2 cup diced avocado; toss gently. Serve hot or at room temperature.
3. Best when served the day of preparation.

SAVORY HAMBURGER SUPPER

Servings: 6 | Prep: 10m | Cooks: 20m | Total: 30m

NUTRITION FACTS

Calories: 350 | Carbohydrates: 41.4g | Fat: 11.5g | Protein: 21.5g | Cholesterol: 52mg

INGREDIENTS

- 1 pound ground beef
- 17 ounces whole kernel corn
- 1/4 cup chopped onion
- 1 (14.5 ounce) can diced tomatoes
- 2 teaspoons chili powder
- 1 (7.25 ounce) package macaroni and cheese mix
- 2 1/4 cups hot water

DIRECTIONS

1. Heat a 3-quart saucepan over medium-high heat. Cook and stir beef and onion in the hot skillet until browned and crumbly, 5 to 7 minutes; drain and discard grease.
2. Return pan to heat and season ground beef mixture with chili powder. Pour water into the saucepan and bring to a boil. Stir corn, tomatoes, and macaroni into the mixture; bring to a simmer and cook until the macaroni is tender, about 10 minutes.
3. Sprinkle contents of cheese packet from macaroni and cheese package over the mixture; stir.

EASY RICE COOKER MAC 'N CHEESE

Servings: 3 | Prep: 10m | Cooks: 30m | Total: 40m

NUTRITION FACTS

Calories: 417 | Carbohydrates: 43.7g | Fat: 16.2g | Protein: 23g | Cholesterol: 50mg

INGREDIENTS

- 1 1/2 cups elbow macaroni
- 1/2 cup shredded mozzarella cheese
- 1 1/2 cups low-sodium chicken broth
- 1/4 cup grated Parmesan cheese
- 1 cup unsweetened almond milk
- 1/4 teaspoon paprika
- 3/4 cup shredded Cheddar cheese
- salt and ground black pepper to taste

1. Mix macaroni, broth, and almond milk together in the rice cooker and cook according to manufacturer's instructions until macaroni is tender yet firm to the bite, 30 to 40 minutes.
2. Stir Cheddar cheese, mozzarella cheese, Parmesan cheese, paprika, salt, and pepper into macaroni mixture until cheeses are melted.

SHIPWRECK DINNER

Servings: 4 | Prep: 10m | Cooks: 20m | Total: 30m

NUTRITION FACTS

Calories: 636 | Carbohydrates: 55g | Fat: 26.7g | Protein: 42.9g | Cholesterol: 116mg

INGREDIENTS

- 1 pound lean ground beef
- 1 cup frozen peas
- 1 (7.25 ounce) package macaroni and cheese mix
- 1 cup frozen corn
- 1 (14.5 ounce) can diced tomatoes
- 1 teaspoon seasoned salt (such as LAWRY'S), or to taste
- 1 cup milk
- 1 cup shredded Cheddar cheese, divided

DIRECTIONS

1. Heat a large skillet over medium-high heat. Cook and stir beef in the hot skillet until browned and crumbly, 5 to 7 minutes.
2. Stir pasta and cheese mixture from the macaroni and cheese package into the beef. Add tomatoes, milk, peas, and corn to the beef mixture; stir. Bring the mixture to a boil, reduce heat to medium-low, place a cover on the skillet and cook at a simmer until the noodles are tender, about 12 minutes.
3. Season the dish with seasoned salt. Stir about half of the Cheddar cheese into dish to melt. Top with remaining cheese.

MEXICAN MAC AND CHEESE

Servings: 8 | Prep: 20m | Cooks: 40m | Total: 1h

NUTRITION FACTS

Calories: 454 | Carbohydrates: 44.4g | Fat: 18.2g | Protein: 26.4g | Cholesterol: 71mg

INGREDIENTS

- 1 1/2 pounds lean ground beef
- 15 ounces nacho cheese dip
- 2 tablespoons dried onion flakes
- 1 cup medium salsa
- 2 (7.25 ounce) packages dry macaroni and cheese
- 1 (7 ounce) can diced green chiles

DIRECTIONS

1. In a medium skillet over medium-high heat, cook beef with onion flakes until beef is browned. Drain.
2. In a large saucepan, cook the macaroni and cheese according to package directions. Stir in the meat and onion mixture, nacho cheese dip, salsa and green chiles. Reduce heat and simmer 15 minutes, or until heated through.

TUNA CHEESE MAC

Servings: 5 | Prep: 5m | Cooks: 20m | Total: 25m

NUTRITION FACTS

Calories: 535 | Carbohydrates: 13.7g | Fat: 35.2g | Protein: 40.3g | Cholesterol: 129mg

INGREDIENTS

- 1 cup uncooked egg noodles
- 1/3 cup cottage cheese
- 2 1/2 cups sharp Cheddar cheese, shredded
- 2 tablespoons sour cream
- 1/4 cup milk
- 1 (12 ounce) can tuna, drained
- 1/4 cup butter
- 1 1/2 cups green peas

DIRECTIONS

1. Bring a large pot of lightly salted water to a boil. Add pasta and cook for 8 to 10 minutes or until al dente; drain.
2. In a saucepan over medium heat, combine cheddar cheese, milk, butter, cottage cheese, and sour cream; stir until melted.
3. Pour cooked noodles into the cheese mixture and stir until well mixed. Stir in canned tuna and green peas; heat thoroughly.

EASY MAC 'N' CHEESE

Servings: 4 | Prep: 2m | Cooks: 13m | Total: 15m

NUTRITION FACTS

Calories: 284 | Carbohydrates: 25.9g | Fat: 14.9g | Protein: 10.8g | Cholesterol: 36mg

INGREDIENTS

- 1 cup macaroni
- 1 teaspoon grated Parmesan cheese
- 1/2 cup process cheese sauce
- 1 pinch dried oregano
- 2 frankfurters, sliced
- 4 buttery round crackers, crushed

DIRECTIONS

1. Preheat oven to 350 degrees F (175 degrees C). Bring a large pot of lightly salted water to a boil. Add pasta and cook for 8 to 10 minutes or until al dente; drain. Heat cheese sauce in microwave, 1 minute. In 8 x 8 inch baking dish, combine cooked pasta, cheese sauce, sliced frankfurters, Parmesan and oregano. Top with crumbled crackers and bake 10 minutes.

CHEESY MACARONI AND HAMBURGER CASSEROLE

Servings: 8 | Prep: 20m | Cooks: 40m | Total: 1h

NUTRITION FACTS

Calories: 689 | Carbohydrates: 50g | Fat: 40g | Protein: 30.7g | Cholesterol: 103mg

INGREDIENTS

- 2 1/2 cups elbow macaroni
- 1 (8 ounce) carton sour cream
- 1 (8 ounce) package processed cheese (such as Velveeta), cubed
- 1/2 cup grated Parmesan cheese
- 1 pound ground beef
- 1/4 cup chopped onion
- 1 teaspoon garlic powder
- 1/4 cup milk
- 1/2 teaspoon onion powder
- 8 slices American cheese (such as Kraft)
- 1 pinch salt and ground black pepper to taste
- 1 (8 ounce) package buttery round crackers (such as Ritz), crushed

- 1 (10.75 ounce) can condensed Cheddar cheese soup (such as Campbell's)

DIRECTIONS

1. Preheat oven to 400 degrees F (200 degrees C). Lightly grease an 11x13-inch baking dish.
2. Bring a large pot of lightly salted water to a boil. Cook elbow macaroni in the boiling water, stirring occasionally until cooked through but firm to the bite, 8 minutes. Drain. Transfer to a bowl, add processed cheese cubes, and let stand until cheese partially melts.
3. Place ground beef in a skillet over medium heat, break meat apart with a spatula, and sprinkle with garlic powder, onion powder, salt, and black pepper. Cook and stir until beef is browned and crumbly, about 10 minutes. Drain excess grease.
4. Stir Cheddar cheese soup, sour cream, Parmesan cheese, and onion together in a bowl; gently fold macaroni and processed cheese mixture into soup mixture. Stir in milk until thoroughly combined. Mix ground beef into macaroni mixture and spread into prepared baking dish. Top casserole with slices of American cheese and sprinkle cracker crumbs on top. Cover casserole with aluminum foil.
5. Bake in the preheated oven until casserole is bubbling, about 20 minutes; remove foil and bake until top is golden brown, about 10 more minutes.

HEALTHIER HOMEMADE MAC AND CHEESE
Servings: 4 | Prep: 20m | Cooks: 30m | Total: 50m

NUTRITION FACTS

Calories: 770 | Carbohydrates: 106.6g | Fat: 22.4g | Protein: 42.5g | Cholesterol: 60mg

INGREDIENTS

- 1 (16 ounce) package whole wheat macaroni (such as Smart Taste)
- 3 cups low-fat (1%) milk
- 2 tablespoons butter
- 2 tablespoons butter
- 2 1/2 tablespoons all-purpose flour
- 1/2 cup whole wheat bread crumbs
- 2 cups shredded low-fat Cheddar cheese
- 1 pinch paprika
- 1/2 cup grated Parmesan cheese

DIRECTIONS

1. Preheat oven to 350 degrees F (175 degrees C). Bring a large pot of lightly salted water to a boil. Cook elbow macaroni in boiling water, stirring occasionally until cooked through but firm to the bite, 8 minutes. Drain.
2. Melt 2 tablespoons butter in a saucepan over medium heat. Stir in flour to make a roux. Slowly add milk to roux, stirring constantly. Stir in Cheddar and Parmesan cheeses and cook over low heat until

cheese is melted and sauce is thick, about 3 minutes. Place macaroni in large baking dish and pour sauce over macaroni. Stir well.

3. Melt 2 tablespoons butter in a skillet over medium heat. Add breadcrumbs and stir until butter is absorbed, 2 to 3 minutes. Spread over macaroni to cover. Sprinkle with paprika.

4. Bake in preheated oven until cheese sauce is hot and breadcrumbs are browned, about 30 minutes.

CHEATING CHEESEBURGER MACARONI
Servings: 8 | Prep: 5m | Cooks: 20m | Total: 25m

NUTRITION FACTS

Calories: 380 | Carbohydrates: 31.3g | Fat: 18.1g | Protein: 21.1g | Cholesterol: 67mg

INGREDIENTS

- 1 (8 ounce) package dry penne pasta
- 1 (10.75 ounce) can condensed cream of chicken soup with herbs
- 1 1/2 pounds ground beef
- 1 (10.75 ounce) can condensed Cheddar cheese soup
- 1/4 cup chopped onion
- 1 cup water
- 1 (10.75 ounce) can condensed cream of onion soup
- 1/4 cup sour cream (optional)

DIRECTIONS

1. Bring a large pot of lightly salted water to a boil. Add penne, and cook for 8 to 10 minutes, or until tender. Drain.

2. Heat a large skillet over medium-high heat. Add ground beef and onion; cook, stirring to crumble the beef, until evenly browned. Drain off excess grease, and mix in the cream of onion soup, cream of chicken soup, and Cheddar cheese soup, along with the water and sour cream. Simmer over medium heat for a few minutes. Stir in the cooked pasta, and serve immediately.

CHURCH SUPPER MACARONI AND CHEESE
Servings: 8 | Prep: 20m | Cooks: 55m | Total: 1h15m

NUTRITION FACTS

Calories: 710 | Carbohydrates: 40.4g | Fat: 47.2g | Protein: 31.7g | Cholesterol: 188mg

INGREDIENTS

- 2 tablespoons salt
- 1/2 (14 ounce) can sweetened condensed milk

- 2 cups elbow macaroni
- 1 1/2 pounds extra-sharp Cheddar cheese, shredded
- 1/4 cup butter, softened
- 1 pinch paprika, or to taste
- 2 large eggs
- 1/4 cup butter (optional)
- 1 (12 fluid ounce) can evaporated milk
- 1/2 cup soft bread crumbs (optional)

DIRECTIONS

1. Preheat oven to 350 degrees F (175 degrees C). Grease a 2-quart casserole with butter.
2. Dissolve salt in a large pot of water. Bring to a boil and cook macaroni, stirring often, until pasta is tender but still slightly firm to the bite, about 8 minutes. Rinse macaroni under cool water, drain, and transfer to a bowl. Stir 1/4 cup softened butter into macaroni and toss a few times to melt butter and coat macaroni.
3. Beat eggs in a bowl; whisk evaporated and condensed milks into eggs.
4. Spread a layer of macaroni into the bottom of the prepared casserole; sprinkle with a layer of Cheddar cheese. Continue layering macaroni and cheese, ending with a layer of cheese on top. Pour egg-milk mixture over the layers. Use a fork to gently dig into the layers, assuring that the egg-milk mixture flows into all the layers. Sprinkle with paprika.
5. Melt 1/4 cup butter in a small skillet over medium heat; cook bread crumbs in the hot butter, stirring constantly, until fragrant and golden, 2 to 3 minutes. Sprinkle crumb topping over casserole.
6. Bake in the preheated oven until casserole is browned and bubbling, about 45 minutes.

BACON WHITE CHEDDAR PESTO MAC AND CHEESE

Servings: 8 | Prep: 10m | Cooks: 35m | Total: 45m

NUTRITION FACTS

Calories: 563 | Carbohydrates: 50.7g | Fat: 30g | Protein: 23.1g | Cholesterol: 76mg

INGREDIENTS

- 1 (16 ounce) package elbow macaroni
- 2 cups milk
- 1/2 cup basil pesto sauce, purchased or homemade
- 1/2 cup heavy cream
- 6 slices bacon
- salt and pepper to taste
- 2 tablespoons butter
- 8 ounces grated white Cheddar cheese
- 2 garlic cloves, minced

- 1/4 cup panko bread crumbs
- 2 tablespoons all-purpose flour
- 1/4 cup grated Parmesan cheese

DIRECTIONS

1. Preheat oven to 350 degrees F (175 degrees C). Grease a 2 1/2- or 3-quart baking dish.
2. Bring a large pot of lightly salted water to a boil. Cook elbow macaroni in the boiling water, stirring occasionally until tender yet firm to the bite, 8 minutes. Drain. Transfer pasta back to pot; cover and keep warm off heat.
3. Place bacon in a large skillet and cook over medium-high heat, turning occasionally, until evenly browned and crisp, about 10 minutes. Drain bacon slices on paper towels. Crumble.
4. Place butter and minced garlic in a saucepan over medium-high heat; stir until butter is melted. Whisk flour into butter mixture, and continue whisking until flour starts to turn golden brown, about 1 minute. Slowly add milk, heavy cream, salt, and pepper to the saucepan, whisking until there are no lumps. Bring to a boil, stirring frequently. Reduce heat to medium.
5. Stir grated Cheddar cheese into the cream mixture, stirring until the cheese is melted. Add basil pesto sauce and half of the crumbled bacon; stir. Transfer mixture to pot with cooked elbows; stir to combine. Pour into prepared baking dish.
6. Mix panko bread crumbs and Parmesan cheese together in a bowl. Sprinkle topping evenly over macaroni and cheese.
7. Bake in preheated oven until bubbly and just starting to brown, about 20 minutes. Top with remaining half of bacon.
8. Preheat the oven's broiler. Place baking dish under broiler until browned, 1 to 3 minutes. Garnish with chopped basil.

MACARONI WITH HAM AND CHEESE DELUXE

Servings: 12 | Prep: 30m | Cooks: 25m | Total: 55m

NUTRITION FACTS

Calories: 453 | Carbohydrates: 32.3g | Fat: 25.3g | Protein: 23.3g | Cholesterol: 75mg

INGREDIENTS

- 1 (16 ounce) package elbow macaroni
- 4 ounces shredded Monterey Jack cheese
- 1/4 cup butter
- 4 ounces shredded hot pepper Monterey Jack cheese
- 1 onion, chopped
- 2 ounces shredded sharp white Cheddar cheese
- 1 teaspoon minced garlic
- 3/4 cup milk, or more as needed

- 1 green bell pepper, chopped
- 4 Italian plum tomatoes, cut into wedges
- 4 cups cubed, fully cooked ham
- 6 ounces shredded sharp white Cheddar cheese

DIRECTIONS

1. Preheat oven to 325 degrees F (165 degrees C).
2. Bring a large pot of lightly salted water to a boil. Cook elbow macaroni in the boiling water, stirring occasionally until cooked through but firm to the bite, 8 minutes. Drain.
3. Melt butter in a Dutch oven over medium heat. Cook and stir onion, garlic, and green bell pepper in melted butter until tender, about 5 minutes.
4. Stir cooked macaroni, ham, Monterey Jack cheese, hot pepper Jack cheese, and 2 ounces sharp white Cheddar cheese into onion mixture until well blended.
5. Gently stir milk into mixture until casserole is creamy, adding additional milk if needed.
6. Stir tomato wedges into casserole. Top with 6 ounces sharp white Cheddar cheese.
7. Bake casserole in the preheated oven until cheese is bubbling and browned on top, about 20 minutes.

HEALTHIER CHUCK'S FAVORITE MAC AND CHEESE

Servings: 6 | Prep: 10m | Cooks: 45m | Total: 55m

NUTRITION FACTS

Calories: 380 | Carbohydrates: 45.9g | Fat: 9.9g | Protein: 28.5g | Cholesterol: 32mg

INGREDIENTS

- 8 ounces whole wheat elbow macaroni
- 1/4 cup grated Parmesan cheese
- 1 (8 ounce) package shredded reduced-fat Cheddar cheese
- salt and ground black pepper to taste
- 12 ounces low-fat cottage cheese
- 1 cup whole wheat bread crumbs
- 1 (8 ounce) container light sour cream
- 2 tablespoons butter, melted

DIRECTIONS

1. Preheat oven to 350 degrees F (175 degrees C).
2. Bring a large pot of lightly salted water to a boil. Cook elbow macaroni in the boiling water, stirring occasionally until cooked through but firm to the bite, 8 minutes. Drain.
3. Stir together macaroni, shredded Cheddar cheese, cottage cheese, sour cream, Parmesan cheese, and salt and pepper in a 9x13-inch baking dish. Mix together bread crumbs and melted butter in a small bowl; sprinkle topping over macaroni mixture.

4. Bake until top is golden in the preheated oven, 30 to 35 minutes.

GOOD FOR YOU MACARONI AND CHEESE
Servings: 8 | Prep: 25m | Cooks: 1h | Total: 1h30m

NUTRITION FACTS

Calories: 624 | Carbohydrates: 65.6g | Fat: 29.5g | Protein: 24g | Cholesterol: 81mg

INGREDIENTS

- 1 (16 ounce) package elbow macaroni
- 1/2 cup canned garbanzo beans, rinsed and drained
- 2 tablespoons butter
- 1/2 cup dry bread crumbs
- 2 tablespoons all-purpose flour
- 1/4 cup grated Parmesan cheese
- 1 (12 fluid ounce) can evaporated milk
- 1 cup mashed sweet potatoes
- 1/2 cup water
- 1 cup sour cream
- 1 pinch red pepper flakes, or to taste
- 2 cups shredded, yellow sharp Cheddar cheese, divided
- 1 pinch ground nutmeg, or to taste
- 1/2 cup shredded, white extra-sharp Cheddar cheese, divided
- salt and pepper to taste
- 2 tablespoons butter

DIRECTIONS

1. Fill a large pot with lightly salted water and bring to a rolling boil over high heat. Once the water is boiling, stir in the macaroni, and return to a boil. Cook the pasta uncovered, stirring occasionally, until the pasta has cooked through, but is still very firm to the bite, about 5 minutes. Drain well in a colander set in the sink, and rinse with cold water until cold; set aside.
2. Meanwhile, melt 2 tablespoons of butter in a large saucepan over medium-low heat. Whisk in the flour, and stir until the mixture becomes paste-like and light golden brown, about 5 minutes. Gradually whisk the evaporated milk and water into the flour mixture, and bring to a simmer over medium heat. Season to taste with red pepper flakes, nutmeg, salt, and pepper. Cook and stir until the mixture is thick and smooth, 10 to 15 minutes.
3. Preheat an oven to 350 degrees F (175 degrees C). Grease a 9x13 inch baking dish.
4. Place the garbanzo beans into a blender. Cover, and puree until smooth. Scrape the puree into a small bowl and stir in the bread crumbs and Parmesan cheese; set aside.
5. Once the sauce has thickened, whisk in the sweet potatoes and sour cream; return to a simmer. Whisk in half of the yellow and white Cheddar cheeses until melted. Stir in the macaroni until well coated with the sauce, then pour half into the prepared baking dish. Sprinkle the remaining Cheddar

cheeses overtop, then cover with the remaining macaroni. Smooth the top, then dot with the garbanzo bean mixture and the remaining 2 tablespoons of butter.

6. Bake in the preheated oven until the sauce is bubbly, and the top is golden brown, 30 to 40 minutes. Allow the dish to rest for 5 minutes before serving.

NOT YOUR MOM'S MAC AND CHEESE

Servings: 8 | Prep: 25m | Cooks: 30m | Total: 55m

NUTRITION FACTS

Calories: 660 | Carbohydrates: 53.9g | Fat: 34g | Protein: 35g | Cholesterol: 115mg

INGREDIENTS

- 1 (16 ounce) package gemelli (small twisted pasta)
- 1/4 cup grated Parmesan cheese
- 1 tablespoon olive oil
- 1/8 teaspoon paprika
- 1 pound lean ground beef
- 1/8 teaspoon ground nutmeg
- salt and ground black pepper to taste
- 1/8 teaspoon garlic powder
- 3 tablespoons butter
- 1 pinch ground cinnamon
- 3 tablespoons all-purpose flour
- 1 pinch chili powder
- 3 cups milk
- 2 tablespoons butter
- 1 cup shredded fontina cheese
- 1/2 cup Italian-seasoned breadcrumbs
- 1 cup shredded sharp Cheddar cheese
- 2 tablespoons grated Parmesan cheese
- 1 cup shredded white Cheddar cheese

DIRECTIONS

1. Fill a large pot with lightly salted water and bring to a rolling boil over high heat. Once the water is boiling, stir in the gemelli, and return to a boil. Cook uncovered, stirring occasionally, until the pasta has cooked through, but is still firm to the bite, about 8 minutes. Drain well in a colander set in the sink. Add olive oil, and toss pasta until coated; set aside.

2. Heat a large skillet over medium-high heat and stir in the ground beef. Season with salt and black pepper. Cook and stir until the beef is crumbly, evenly browned, and no longer pink, about 10 minutes. Drain and discard any excess grease. Set aside.

3. Preheat an oven to 350 degrees F (175 degrees C).
4. Heat 3 tablespoons butter and the flour in a large skillet over low heat. Cook and stir until the butter is melted and the flour is incorporated, then slowly whisk in the milk. Stir in the fontina cheese, sharp Cheddar cheese, white Cheddar cheese, and 1/4 cup Parmesan cheese; cook, whisking constantly, until cheese is melted and sauce is thickened, about 5 minutes. Season with paprika, nutmeg, garlic powder, cinnamon, and chili powder. Season to taste with salt and black pepper. Stir in the pasta and beef, and transfer mixture to a large baking dish.
5. Combine 2 tablespoons butter, bread crumbs, and the remaining 2 tablespoons Parmesan cheese in a bowl. Sprinkle mixture over the pasta in the baking dish.
6. Bake in the preheated oven until bubbly, about 12 minutes, then set the oven on broil. Broil until lightly browned, about 3 more minutes.

SLOW COOKER MACARONI AND CHEESE

Servings: 8 | Prep: 15m | Cooks:4h | Total: 4h15m

NUTRITION FACTS

Calories: 438 | Carbohydrates: 29.5g | Fat: 27.9g | Protein: 17.3g | Cholesterol: 89mg

INGREDIENTS

- 2 cups macaroni or pasta of choice, uncooked
- 1 cup milk
- 3 tablespoons butter
- 1/2 cup whipping cream
- 8 ounces processed American cheese, cubed
- 1 (12 ounce) can evaporated milk
- 8 ounces light cream cheese, cubed
- 1 (10 ounce) can RED GOLD Petite Diced Tomatoes & Green Chilies, drained
- 1 teaspoon Dijon mustard

DIRECTIONS

1. Place the uncooked pasta in the bottom of a 3.5 quart slow cooker that has been sprayed with cooking spray. Add the remaining ingredients, except tomatoes, to the slow cooker and stir until well combined. Cook on LOW for 4 hours.
2. Just before serving add tomatoes; stir to combine.

SOUTHWESTERN MACARONI AND CHEESE WITH ADOBO MEATBALLS

Servings: 8 | Prep: 25m | Cooks: 40m | Total: 1h5m

Calories: 589 | Carbohydrates: 29.2g | Fat: 36.4g | Protein: 35.7g | Cholesterol: 121mg

INGREDIENTS

- 1 (8 ounce) package elbow macaroni
- 1 cup light sour cream
- 3/4 pound lean ground beef
- 4 cups shredded Cheddar cheese
- 3 tablespoons adobo seasoning
- 2 cups fat-free cottage cheese
- 2 teaspoons powdered jalapeno pepper
- 1/2 cup crumbled cotija cheese
- 2 teaspoons olive oil
- 1/2 teaspoon garlic powder
- 2 teaspoons butter
- 2 tablespoons chopped fresh cilantro
- 1/4 cup cream
- salt and white pepper to taste
- 1 cup canned diced green chiles

DIRECTIONS

1. Preheat oven to 325 degrees F (165 degrees C). Bring a large pot of lightly salted water to a boil. Add macaroni and cook for 8 to 10 minutes or until al dente; drain.
2. In a large bowl, mix ground beef with adobo seasoning and powdered jalapeno pepper. Roll into small, 1 inch meatballs. Heat olive oil in a large skillet over medium-high heat. Add meatballs, and cook until browned on all sides, then remove to drain on a paper towel-lined plate. The meatballs do not need to be thoroughly cooked at this point as they will finish cooking in the oven.
3. While the meatballs are cooking, melt the butter in a large saucepan over medium heat. Gently cook the butter until it begins to brown, and acquires a nutty fragrance, about 1 minute. Stir in the cream, sour cream, Cheddar cheese, cottage cheese, cotija cheese, garlic powder, and cilantro. Bring to a simmer, stirring constantly until the cheese has melted. Season to taste with salt and white pepper.
4. Stir the cooked macaroni and diced chiles into the cheese sauce, and pour into a 9x13 inch baking dish. Slice the meatballs in half, and place onto the pasta cut-side down.
5. Bake in preheated oven until the cheese sauce is bubbly, and the meatballs are no longer pink in the center, about 25 minutes.

CREOLE MACARONI AND CHEESE

Servings: 8 | Prep: 25m | Cooks: 20m | Total: 45m

NUTRITION FACTS

Calories: 481 | Carbohydrates: 34g | Fat: 28.6g | Protein: 21.5g | Cholesterol: 77mg

INGREDIENTS

- 1 (8 ounce) package elbow macaroni
- 1/2 teaspoon paprika
- 1 cup andouille sausage, diced
- 1/2 teaspoon prepared mustard
- 4 tablespoons butter
- 1 1/2 cups milk
- 3/4 cup bread crumbs
- 1 cup grated Gruyere cheese
- 1/2 cup grated Parmesan cheese
- 1 1/2 cups shredded Cheddar cheese
- 1 onion, chopped
- kosher salt to taste
- 2 stalks celery, chopped
- black pepper to taste
- 1 tablespoon all-purpose flour

DIRECTIONS

1. Cook macaroni in a large pot of boiling water until al dente. Drain.
2. In a small pan, cook the andouille sausage over medium heat until done. Set aside. In the same pan, melt 1 tablespoon butter over medium heat. Add bread crumbs, and stir to coat. Cool, and then mix in Parmesan. Set aside.
3. In a medium saucepan, melt 1 tablespoon butter. Saute onions and celery until translucent. Transfer to a bowl.
4. In the same saucepan, melt 1 tablespoon butter over medium heat. Whisk in the flour, to make a white roux. Try not to let the roux brown at all, it should be white. Mix in paprika and mustard, then stir in milk. Bring to boil over medium heat, then add Gruyere and Cheddar cheeses. Simmer, stirring often, until thick enough to coat the back of a spoon, about 10 minutes. Season with salt and pepper to taste.
5. Preheat the oven to 350 degrees F (175 degrees C). Butter a 9x13 in pan, or similar sized casserole dish. Transfer cooked macaroni to the dish, and toss in the andouille sausage and sauteed vegetables. Stir in the cheese mixture. Sprinkle the breadcrumb and Parmesan mixture evenly over the top.
6. Bake for 20 minutes, or until crust turns golden brown.

RANCH MAC 'N CHEESE
Servings: 6 | Prep: 10m | Cooks: 20 | Total: 30m

NUTRITION FACTS

Calories: 701 | Carbohydrates: 51.7g | Fat: 43.1g | Protein: 27.1g | Cholesterol: 140mg

INGREDIENTS

- 3 cups gemelli pasta, uncooked
- 3 cups grated Asiago cheese
- 1 (5 ounce) can evaporated milk
- 1/2 cup unseasoned bread crumbs
- 1 cup Hidden Valley Original Ranch Salad Dressing
- 2 tablespoons unsalted butter
- 2 eggs, slightly beaten

DIRECTIONS

1. Preheat oven to 350 degrees F.
2. Cook pasta according to package directions. Rinse and drain.
3. In a medium bowl, whisk evaporated milk, dressing and eggs together until smooth. Fold in the cheese. Add the cooked pasta and mix well. Spoon pasta mixture into an oiled 1 1/2-quart casserole. In a bowl, combine bread crumbs and melted butter. Sprinkle on top of pasta. Bake for 20 to 25 minutes until the top is nicely browned and heated through.

MACARONI AND CHEESE CASSEROLE

Servings: 8 | Prep: 15m | Cooks: 25m | Total: 40m

NUTRITION FACTS

Calories: 525 | Carbohydrates: 33.9g | Fat: 32.8g | Protein: 22.8g | Cholesterol: 83mg

INGREDIENTS

- 1 (8 ounce) package uncooked elbow macaroni
- 1 (10.75 ounce) can condensed cream of mushroom soup
- 1 pound processed cheese, cubed
- 1 pound kielbasa sausage, sliced
- 1 (15 ounce) can mixed vegetables, drained

DIRECTIONS

1. Preheat oven to 350 degrees F (175 degrees C).
2. Bring a large pot of lightly salted water to a boil. Add macaroni and cook for 8 to 10 minutes or until al dente; drain.
3. In a large bowl combine macaroni, processed cheese, mixed vegetables, mushroom soup, 1/2 of a soup can of water and sausage. Transfer to a 9x13 inch baking dish.
4. Bake, covered with aluminum foil, for 20 to 25 minutes.

MOM'S MACARONI AND CHEESE
Servings: 8 | Prep: 10m | Cooks: 30m | Total: 40m

NUTRITION FACTS

Calories: 869 | Carbohydrates: 94.9g | Fat: 38.8g | Protein: 35.3g | Cholesterol: 73mg

INGREDIENTS

- 1 pound elbow macaroni
- 1/2 teaspoon ground black pepper
- 1/2 cup vegetable oil
- 1 pound American cheese, cubed
- 2 cups all-purpose flour
- 1 (28 ounce) can crushed tomatoes
- 2 quarts milk
- ¾ cup seasoned dry bread crumbs

DIRECTIONS

1. Preheat oven to 450 degrees F (230 degrees C). Bring a large pot of lightly salted water to a boil. Add pasta and cook for 5 to 7 minutes or until just less than al dente; drain.
2. In large saucepan, heat oil over medium heat. Add flour all at once and stir vigorously until combined. Add milk a little at a time, stirring constantly until all milk is incorporated and sauce is smooth. Stir in pepper, American cheese and tomatoes. Stir until cheese is melted and mixture is smooth (if cheese starts to stick, reduce heat). Place macaroni in a 10x15 baking dish. Pour cheese mixture over macaroni, and sprinkle with bread crumbs.
3. Bake 15 minutes, or until top is golden.

JULIE'S FAMOUS MACARONI AND CHEESE
Servings: 16 | Prep: 30m | Cooks: 45m | Total: 1h15m

NUTRITION FACTS

Calories: 602 | Carbohydrates: 44.1g | Fat: 37.3g | Protein: 23.1g | Cholesterol: 108mg

INGREDIENTS

- 1 (16 ounce) package elbow macaroni
- 4 (12 fluid ounce) cans evaporated milk
- 3/4 cup butter
- 8 ounces shredded sharp Cheddar cheese
- 1 teaspoon salt
- 8 ounces processed cheese food (such as Velveeta), cubed

- 1/2 teaspoon ground black pepper
- 8 ounces shredded Colby Jack cheese
- 2 teaspoons ground dry mustard
- 1 cup small curd cottage cheese
- 1 large yellow onion, minced
- 1/2 cup butter
- 3/4 cup all-purpose flour
- 1 (5.5 ounce) package seasoned croutons (such as New York Brand Texas Toast Sea Salt and Pepper)

DIRECTIONS

1. Preheat oven to 350 degrees F (175 degrees C).
2. Fill a large pot with lightly salted water and bring to a rolling boil over high heat. Once the water is boiling, stir in the macaroni, and return to a boil. Cook the pasta uncovered, stirring occasionally, until the pasta has cooked through, but is still firm to the bite, about 8 minutes. Drain well in a colander set in the sink.
3. Melt 3/4 cup of butter in a saucepan over medium heat, and stir in salt, black pepper, and dry mustard. Add the onion, stir a few times to coat with butter, and cook until translucent, stirring occasionally, about 5 minutes. Gradually stir in the flour, and mix until smoothly combined with the butter. Gradually pour in the evaporated milk, and whisk until the sauce is thickened and bubbly, about 5 more minutes.
4. Stirring constantly, mix in the Cheddar cheese, processed cheese, and Colby Jack cheese until the cheeses have melted and incorporated into the sauce. Stir in the cottage cheese. Mix the cheese mixture with the cooked macaroni in a large bowl, then pour into a large foil baking pan.
5. Melt 1/2 cup of butter in a large skillet, and toss the seasoned croutons with the butter until thoroughly coated. Press the buttered croutons into the top of the macaroni and cheese.
6. Bake in the preheated oven until the casserole is bubbly and the croutons have turned golden brown, about 30 minutes.

VINCENTE'S MACARONI AND CHEESE
Servings: 4 | Prep: 10m | Cooks: 25m | Total: 35m

NUTRITION FACTS

Calories: 463 | Carbohydrates: 50.7g | Fat: 19.3g | Protein: 20.9g | Cholesterol: 57mg

INGREDIENTS

- 1 (8 ounce) box elbow macaroni
- 1/4 teaspoon salt
- 1 tablespoon butter
- 1 cup milk

- 1 small onion, chopped
- 1 1/2 cups grated sharp Cheddar cheese
- 2 tablespoons all-purpose flour
- 1 pinch ground black pepper
- 1 teaspoon dry mustard

DIRECTIONS

1. Fill a large pot with lightly salted water and bring to a rolling boil over high heat. Once the water is boiling, stir in the macaroni, and return to a boil. Cook the pasta uncovered, stirring occasionally, until the pasta has cooked through, but is still firm to the bite, about 8 minutes. Drain well in a colander set in the sink.
2. Melt the butter in a skillet over medium heat. Stir in the onion; cook and stir until the onion has softened and turned translucent, about 5 minutes. Reduce heat to low, then stir in the flour, mustard, and salt until thoroughly combined. Gradually stir in the milk, then increase heat to medium-high and simmer until thickened, stirring constantly, about 3 minutes.
3. Stir in the Cheddar cheese and black pepper until cheese is melted and the sauce is smooth, about 3 minutes. Stir in the macaroni until well-coated and heated through.

BEST EVER MAC AND CHEESE

Servings: 6 | Prep: 15m | Cooks: 45m | Total: 1h

NUTRITION FACTS

Calories: 730 | Carbohydrates: 61.7g | Fat: 40.3g | Protein: 30.1g | Cholesterol: 108mg

INGREDIENTS

- 1 (16 ounce) package elbow macaroni
- 1 (8 ounce) package shredded Cheddar cheese
- 1 (16 ounce) package cottage cheese
- 1 (10 ounce) can whole peeled tomatoes with juice
- 1 cup sour cream
- salt and ground black pepper to taste
- 1/2 cup butter

DIRECTIONS

1. Preheat oven to 350 degrees F (175 degrees C).
2. Fill a large pot with lightly salted water and bring to a rolling boil over high heat. Once the water is boiling, stir in the macaroni, and return to a boil. Cook the pasta uncovered, stirring occasionally, until macaroni is cooked through but still slightly firm, about 8 minutes. Drain well.

3. Combine the cottage cheese, sour cream, butter, and cooked macaroni in a large baking dish. Stir in the Cheddar cheese. Arrange the tomatoes on top, then pour the tomato liquid over the casserole. Season with salt and black pepper.

4. Bake in the preheated oven for 20 minutes, then mix the macaroni and cheese thoroughly. Continue to bake until lightly browned and bubbly, about 15 minutes more.

MENA'S BAKED MACARONI AND CHEESE WITH CARAMELIZED ONION

Servings: 6 | Prep: 20m | Cooks: 1h15m | Total: 1h45m | Additional: 10m

NUTRITION FACTS

Calories: 558 | Carbohydrates: 51.2g | Fat: 29g | Protein: 22.6g | Cholesterol: 82mg

INGREDIENTS

- 6 tablespoons butter, divided
- 1 clove garlic, minced
- 1 large Vidalia or other sweet onion, thinly sliced
- 1 pinch cayenne pepper
- 1/2 teaspoon sugar
- 3 tablespoons all-purpose flour
- 1 pinch salt
- 1 3/4 cups milk
- 1 (8 ounce) box uncooked macaroni
- 3/4 cup low-sodium chicken broth
- 1 cup plain bread crumbs
- 8 ounces grated sharp white Cheddar cheese
- 1/2 teaspoon dried mustard
- 1/2 cup grated Parmesan cheese
- salt and black pepper to taste

DIRECTIONS

1. Preheat oven to 400 degrees F (200 degrees C). Butter a 9x13-inch baking dish.
2. Melt 2 tablespoons of the butter in a large skillet over medium heat. Add onions, sugar, and salt. Cook, stirring often, until onions are caramel colored, 15 to 20 minutes. If mixture is too dry, add an additional tablespoon of butter. Set aside.
3. Bring a large pot of lightly salted water to a boil. Add macaroni and cook until al dente, 8 to 10 minutes. Drain, cover and set aside.
4. Melt 1 tablespoon of the butter in a small skillet over medium heat. Stir in the bread crumbs and toast lightly for a few minutes, stirring constantly.

5. Melt the remaining 3 tablespoons butter in a large pot over medium heat. Dissolve the dry mustard in an equal amount of water and add to the pot along with the garlic, and cayenne pepper. Stir until fragrant, about 30 seconds. Sprinkle in the flour and cook until golden, about 1 minute. Slowly whisk in the milk and broth. Bring to a simmer stirring constantly until the mixture is slightly thickened, about 5 minutes.

6. Remove the pan from the heat and stir in the Cheddar and Parmesan cheeses until melted. Stir in the onions and season with salt and pepper. Add the drained macaroni and stir until blended. Pour into the prepared baking dish and top with bread crumbs.

7. Bake until golden brown and bubbling around the edges, 25 to 30 minutes. Let cool for 10 minutes before serving.

OLD-FASHIONED MACARONI, TOMATO, AND CHEESE BAKE

Servings: 12 | Prep: 15m | Cooks: 53m | Total: 1h8m

NUTRITION FACTS

Calories: 311 | Carbohydrates: 24.4g | Fat: 17.2g | Protein: 14.4g | Cholesterol: 95mg

INGREDIENTS

- 3 cups elbow macaroni
- 1 teaspoon brown mustard
- 3 tablespoons butter, melted
- 2 dashes hot sauce (such as Tabasco)
- 2 cups shredded sharp Cheddar cheese
- 1/2 cup chopped fresh parsley
- 1 (14.5 ounce) can petite diced tomatoes in juice
- 1/4 teaspoon ground nutmeg
- 3 large eggs
- 1 tablespoon ground black pepper
- 2 1/2 cups milk
- 1 teaspoon salt
- 1 (4 ounce) package cream cheese, softened
- 1/4 teaspoon paprika, or to taste
- 1/3 cup grated Parmesan cheese

DIRECTIONS

1. Preheat an oven to 350 degrees F (175 degrees C). Prepare an 8 quart baking dish with cooking spray.
2. Fill a large pot with lightly salted water and bring to a rolling boil over high heat. Once the water is boiling, stir in the macaroni, and return to a boil. Cook the pasta uncovered, stirring occasionally,

until the pasta has cooked through, but is still firm to the bite, about 8 minutes. Drain well in a colander set in the sink. Pour into the prepared baking dish and add the butter, Cheddar cheese, and diced tomatoes; stir.

3. Combine the eggs, milk, cream cheese, Parmesan cheese, brown mustard, hot sauce, parsley, nutmeg, pepper, and salt in a food processor; pulse until smooth; pour over the macaroni. Sprinkle paprika over everything.

4. Bake in the preheated oven until the middle is set, 45 to 50 minutes.

GROWN UP MAC & CHEESE

Servings: 5 | Prep: 10m | Cooks: 15m | Total: 25m

NUTRITION FACTS

Calories: 570 | Carbohydrates: 40.3g | Fat: 37.8g | Protein: 23.3g | Cholesterol: 86mg

INGREDIENTS

- 2 cups uncooked whole grain elbow macaroni
- 1 cup panko bread crumbs
- 2 tablespoons olive oil
- 1 tablespoon chopped fresh parsley
- 3 tablespoons butter
- 8 ounces processed American cheese, cubed
- 3 tablespoons flour
- 1 link Johnsonville Smoked or Three-Cheese Italian Style Premium Cooking Sausage (from 13.5 oz. pkg.), quartered and sliced
- 1 cup fat-free milk

DIRECTIONS

1. Cook macaroni according to package directions; drain.
2. Mix panko, parsley, and olive oil together in a bowl.
3. Meanwhile, in another saucepan, melt butter over medium heat.
4. Stir in flour until smooth; gradually whisk in milk.
5. Bring to a boil, stirring constantly. Cook and stir for 2 minutes or until thickened.
6. Add cheese; cook and stir until melted.
7. Stir in macaroni and sausage.
8. Spread panko mixture on top and bake at 350 degrees F for 25 minutes.
9. Enjoy.

GLUTEN-FREE MACARONI AND THREE CHEESES WITH BACON

Servings: 10 | Prep: 15m | Cooks: 30m | Total: 45m

NUTRITION FACTS

Calories: 587 | Carbohydrates: 38.1g | Fat: 39.2g | Protein: 21.3g | Cholesterol: 141mg

INGREDIENTS

- 16 ounces gluten-free elbow pasta
- 8 ounces shredded fontina cheese
- 2 cups heavy whipping cream
- 8 ounces shredded Gouda cheese
- salt and ground black pepper to taste
- 8 slices cooked bacon, chopped (optional)
- 8 ounces shredded Cheddar cheese

DIRECTIONS

1. Preheat oven to 350 degrees F (175 degrees C). Grease a 9x13-inch baking dish
2. Bring a large pot of lightly salted water to a boil. Cook elbow macaroni in the boiling water, stirring occasionally, until cooked through but firm to the bite, 8 minutes. Drain.
3. Pour cream into a large saucepan over medium heat and season with salt and pepper.
4. Measure about 2 tablespoons Cheddar cheese, 2 tablespoons fontina cheese, and 2 tablespoons Gouda cheese; set aside. Stir remaining Cheddar cheese, fontina cheese, and Gouda cheese into cream; cook, stirring frequently, until cheeses are melted and cheese sauce is smooth, about 5 minutes. Remove saucepan from heat.
5. Mix pasta into cheese sauce until evenly coated; fold in bacon. Pour macaroni and cheese into the prepared baking dish and top with reserved cheese mixture.
6. Bake in the preheated oven until cheese is melted and bubbling, about 15 minutes.

MACARONI AND CHEESE PIZZA BAKE

Servings: 8 | Prep: 15m | Cooks: 40m | Total: 55m

NUTRITION FACTS

Calories: 519 | Carbohydrates: 41.9g | Fat: 27.9g | Protein: 24.8g | Cholesterol: 127mg

INGREDIENTS

- 2 (7.25 ounce) packages macaroni and cheese mix
- 3 cups shredded mozzarella cheese, divided
- 1/2 cup butter

- 1 (16 ounce) jar pizza sauce (such as Prego Traditional Italian Sauce)
- 1/2 cup milk
- 1 (4 ounce) package sliced pepperoni, or to taste
- 2 eggs, beaten
- dried oregano, or to taste

DIRECTIONS

1. Preheat oven to 350 degrees F (175 degrees C). Grease a 9x13-inch baking dish.
2. Bring a large pot of lightly salted water to a boil. Cook elbow macaroni in the boiling water, stirring occasionally until cooked through but firm to the bite, about 8 minutes. Drain and return pasta to pot. Add butter, milk, and cheese mix to macaroni; stir until evenly mixed.
3. Stir eggs into macaroni and cheese until incorporated. Add 1 cup mozzarella cheese; stir until just combined.
4. Spread macaroni and cheese mixture into the prepared baking dish; top with pasta sauce. Sprinkle the remaining 2 cups mozzarella cheese over sauce. Cover the cheese layer with pepperoni and season with oregano.
5. Bake in the preheated oven until cheese is melted, about 30 minutes.

CHEESY SALSA MAC

Servings: 6 | Prep: 10m | Cooks: 30m | Total: 40m

NUTRITION FACTS

Calories: 487 | Carbohydrates: 30.4g | Fat: 26.2g | Protein: 32.1g | Cholesterol: 103mg

INGREDIENTS

- 1 pound ground beef (80% lean)
- 1 1/2 cups elbow macaroni
- 2 cups fresh salsa
- 1 cup milk
- 1 teaspoon taco seasoning mix
- 1 (8 ounce) package processed cheese food (such as Velveeta), cut into cubes
- 1/8 teaspoon ground black pepper
- 4 ounces shredded sharp Cheddar cheese
- 1 1/2 cups hot water

DIRECTIONS

1. Heat a large, deep skillet over medium-high heat. Cook and stir beef in the hot skillet until browned and crumbly, 5 to 7 minutes; drain and discard grease.
2. Return skillet to heat. Stir salsa, taco seasoning mix, and black pepper into the beef; simmer the mixture until hot, about 5 minutes.

3. Stir water, macaroni, and milk into the beef mixture; bring to a boil, reduce heat to medium-low, place a cover on the skillet, and simmer the mixture until the pasta is tender, about 10 minutes.
4. Stir cheese food and Cheddar cheese into the pasta mixture; cook until the cheese melts completely, 5 to 7 minutes.

REUBEN MAC AND CHEESE
Servings: 8 | Prep: 15m | Cooks: 45m | Total: 1h

NUTRITION FACTS

Calories: 583 | Carbohydrates: 56.6g | Fat: 27.6g | Protein: 28.6g | Cholesterol: 127mg

INGREDIENTS

- 3 slices rye bread, torn
- 1/4 cup spicy brown mustard
- 1/3 cup panko bread crumbs
- 3 tablespoons all-purpose flour
- 1 (16 ounce) package egg noodles
- 3 cups hot milk
- 3 tablespoons butter
- 3 cups shredded Swiss cheese, or more to taste - divided
- 1 cup chopped onion
- 1 1/2 cups sauerkraut, drained (reserve juice)
- 1 teaspoon salt
- 1/2 pound deli sliced corn beef, or more to taste
- 1/2 teaspoon ground black pepper
- 3 tablespoons butter, melted

DIRECTIONS

1. Preheat oven to 350 degrees F (175 degrees C). Butter a 2-quart casserole dish.
2. Place torn rye bread into a food processor and pulse several times to make crumbs; combine rye crumbs with panko crumbs in a bowl and set aside.
3. Bring a large pot of lightly salted water to a boil. Cook egg noodles in the boiling water, stirring occasionally until cooked through but firm to the bite, about 5 minutes. Drain noodles and set aside.
4. Melt 3 tablespoons butter in a large saucepan over medium heat; cook and stir onion until lightly browned, about 15 minutes. Season with salt and black pepper; stir in brown mustard. Remove from heat, stir in flour until smooth, and gradually whisk in milk. Sauce will thicken. Whisk 1 1/2 cup Swiss cheese into the sauce, stirring until the cheese has melted and the sauce is smooth. Stir sauerkraut with about 1 tablespoon of reserved juice and corned beef into the cheese sauce.
5. Transfer cooked noodles to the prepared casserole dish and pour in the sauce; stir to combine. Sprinkle remaining 1 1/2 cup Swiss cheese in an even layer over the top.

6. Bake casserole in the preheated oven until bubbling, about 20 minutes. Remove casserole from oven and set the oven to broil.
7. Stir 3 tablespoons melted butter into the reserved rye and panko crumbs until thoroughly combined and sprinkle top of casserole with rye crumb mixture. Return to oven and broil until the crumbs are golden brown, about 2 more minutes. Watch carefully to prevent burning.

NO-BAKE CRISPY POTATO CHIP MAC AND CHEESE

Servings: 2 | Prep: 30m | Cooks: 20m | Total: 50m

NUTRITION FACTS

Calories: 2379 | Carbohydrates: 148.6g | Fat: 162.5g | Protein: 84.9g | Cholesterol: 244mg

INGREDIENTS

- 1 cup elbow macaroni, uncooked
- 4 cups prepared white sauce (see footnote)
- 1 (8 ounce) bag white cheddar kettle-style potato chips, crushed into medium-fine crumbs
- 1/2 pound shredded extra-sharp Cheddar cheese
- 1/3 cup finely grated Parmigiano-Reggiano
- 1/4 pound shredded Gruyere cheese
- 2 tablespoons plain dry bread crumbs
- 1/4 teaspoon dry mustard
- 1 tablespoon butter

DIRECTIONS

1. Bring a large pot of lightly salted water to a boil. Cook elbow macaroni in the boiling water, stirring occasionally until cooked through but firm to the bite, 8 minutes. Drain.
2. Combine potato chip crumbs, Parmigiano-Reggiano cheese, bread crumbs, and butter in a skillet over medium heat; cook and stir until golden brown, about 5 minutes. Set aside.
3. Heat prepared white sauce, Cheddar cheese, Gruyere cheese, and dry mustard in a large saucepan over low heat; cook and stir until cheese melts, 3 to 4 minutes. Remove from heat.
4. Combine cooked macaroni with enough cheese sauce to make it as creamy as you like it (see Cook's Note). Spoon mixture into 2 (10-ounce) ramekins or bowls and cover with toasted potato chip topping.

PUMPKIN LOBSTER MAC AND CHEESE

Servings: 12 | Prep: 15m | Cooks: 1h15m | Total: 1h30m

NUTRITION FACTS

Calories: 427 | Carbohydrates: 33.9g | Fat: 23.6g | Protein: 22.6g | Cholesterol: 83mg

INGREDIENTS

- 1 (12 ounce) package uncooked shell pasta
- 1 pinch garlic powder, or to taste
- 2 tablespoons margarine
- 1 pinch paprika, or to taste
- 1 tablespoon minced shallot
- 1 pinch ground nutmeg, or to taste
- 1 tablespoon all-purpose flour
- 2 dashes hot sauce, or to taste
- 1 (12 fluid ounce) can evaporated milk
- 1 pound cooked lobster tails, peeled and chopped
- 1 (8 ounce) package shredded Cheddar cheese
- 1 (12 ounce) package green peas, thawed if frozen
- 1 (8 ounce) container mascarpone cheese
- 1/2 cup panko bread crumbs
- 1 cup canned pumpkin puree
- 1/3 cup grated Parmesan cheese
- 1 teaspoon lemon zest
- 2 tablespoons margarine, melted
- salt and ground black pepper to taste

DIRECTIONS

1. Bring a large pot of lightly salted water to a rolling boil. Cook pasta shells at a boil until tender but still slightly firm, about 10 minutes; drain and set aside.
2. Preheat the oven to 375 degrees F (190 degrees C).
3. Grease a 9x13-inch casserole dish.
4. Melt 2 tablespoons margarine in a skillet over medium heat. Cook and stir shallot in melted margarine until lightly browned, about 5 minutes.
5. Whisk flour into margarine and shallots to form a smooth paste.
6. Slowly whisk evaporated milk into flour mixture until it forms a smooth sauce; simmer until thickened, 2 to 4 minutes.
7. Whisk shredded Cheddar cheese and mascarpone cheese into sauce until cheeses have melted, about 5 minutes.
8. Stir pumpkin puree, lemon zest, salt, black pepper, garlic powder, paprika, nutmeg, and hot sauce into the sauce until combined.
9. Lightly mix in lobster tail meat, green peas, and cooked pasta shells until heated through, about 5 minutes.
10. Pour pasta mixture into prepared casserole dish; top with panko crumbs and Parmesan cheese. Drizzle 2 tablespoons of melted margarine over the casserole.
11. Bake in the preheated oven until topping is brown and crisp, 40 minutes.

MACARONI AND CHEESE WITH BACON

Servings: 12 | Prep: 20m | Cooks: 30m | Total: 50m

NUTRITION FACTS

Calories: 478 | Carbohydrates: 33.2g | Fat: 30.9g | Protein: 16.5g | Cholesterol: 66mg

INGREDIENTS

- 1 (16 ounce) package rotini pasta
- 1/4 cup butter
- 1 (1 pound) loaf processed cheese food (such as Velveeta), cubed
- 1 pound bacon
- 2 cups tomato juice

DIRECTIONS

1. Preheat oven to 375 degrees F (190 degrees C). Grease a 9x13 inch baking dish.
2. Bring a large pot of water to a boil over high heat. Stir in the rotini, and return to a boil. Cook until the pasta is slightly under-cooked, about 8 minutes. Drain well.
3. Combine the processed cheese, tomato juice, and butter in a large saucepan over medium-high heat. Stir until melted and smooth. Mix the pasta into the cheese sauce; stir well. Transfer macaroni and cheese to the prepared baking dish. Top with the raw bacon slices.
4. Bake in preheated oven until the bacon is cooked and crisped, about 30 minutes.

CLASSIC SMOKED SAUSAGE MAC AND CHEESE

Servings: 10 | Prep: 15m | Cooks: 1h | Total: 1h15m

NUTRITION FACTS

Calories: 922 | Carbohydrates: 56.5g | Fat: 64.3g | Protein: 36g | Cholesterol: 167mg

INGREDIENTS

- 1 pound cavatappi (corkscrew) pasta, uncooked
- 3 cups cubed pasteurized prepared cheese product
- 1 tablespoon butter
- 2 cups shredded sharp Cheddar cheese
- 1 (14 ounce) package Butterball Smoked Turkey Dinner Sausage, halved lengthwise, and cut into 1/4-inch-thick slices
- 1/2 teaspoon ground black pepper
- 1 cup chopped onions
- Cooking spray
- 3 cups prepared Alfredo sauce
- 1 cup panko bread crumbs
- 3 cups half and half
- 1/4 cup butter, melted

DIRECTIONS

1. Preheat oven to 375 degrees F.

2. Cook pasta according to package directions; rinse and drain. Set aside.

3. Melt 1 tablespoon butter in large saucepan on medium heat. Cook and stir sausage and onions 3 to 5 minutes or until onions are tender. Stir in Alfredo sauce, and half and half. Bring to boiling, stirring constantly; reduce heat. Simmer 1 minute.

4. Remove saucepan from heat. Stir in cheese and black pepper until cheese is melted. Stir in pasta and sausage mixture.

5. Pour mixture into lightly sprayed 139-inch baking dish. Sprinkle evenly with combined bread crumbs and 1/4 cup melted butter. Bake 20 to 25 minutes or until crumbs are golden brown and pasta mixture is hot and bubbly.

INSTANT POT MAC AND CHEESE
Servings: 10 | Prep: 5m | Cooks: 15m | Total: 40m

NUTRITION FACTS

Calories: 333 | Carbohydrates: 35.9g | Fat: 13.8g | Protein: 15.7g | Cholesterol: 39mg

INGREDIENTS

- 1 (16 ounce) package elbow macaroni
- 1/2 teaspoon ground black pepper
- 1 quart chicken stock
- 1/2 teaspoon garlic powder
- 1/2 teaspoon salt
- 2 tablespoons butter
- 1/2 teaspoon dry mustard
- 1 cup milk
- 1/2 teaspoon liquid smoke flavoring
- 8 ounces shredded Cheddar cheese
- 1/2 teaspoon paprika
- 1 cup grated Parmesan cheese

DIRECTIONS

1. Combine macaroni, chicken stock, salt, dry mustard, liquid smoke, paprika, pepper, and garlic powder in a multi-functional pressure cooker (such as Instant Pot(R)). Close and lock the lid. Select high pressure according to manufacturer's instructions; set timer for 4 minutes. Allow 10 to 15 minutes for pressure to build.

2. Release pressure carefully using the quick-release method according to manufacturer's instructions, about 5 minutes. Unlock and remove the lid. Stir in butter, milk, Cheddar cheese, and Parmesan cheese until melted. Mixture will be soupy at first.

3. Select the "Keep Warm" setting on the Instant Pot(R) and allow macaroni to sit, uncovered and stirring occasionally, until all liquid has been absorbed and consistency is smooth and creamy, about 15 minutes.

GARLIC CHICKEN MAC AND CHEESE

Servings: 8 | Prep: 15m | Cooks: 1h10m | Total: 1h25m

NUTRITION FACTS

Calories: 851 | Carbohydrates: 69.3g | Fat: 44.9g | Protein: 41.1g | Cholesterol: 138mg

INGREDIENTS

- cooking spray
- 1/4 cup all-purpose flour
- 4 skinless, boneless chicken breast halves, cut into cubes
- 4 cups whole milk
- 2 tablespoons garlic powder, or to taste, divided
- 1 pound Cheddar cheese, shredded
- 1 (16 ounce) package macaroni
- 2 sleeves buttery round crackers (such as Ritz), crushed
- 1/2 cup butter, divided

DIRECTIONS

1. Preheat oven to 450 degrees F (230 degrees C).
2. Prepare a large skillet with cooking spray and place over medium heat. Cook chicken in skillet until no longer pink in the center, 5 to 7 minutes; season with 1 tablespoon garlic powder and transfer to a baking dish.
3. Bring a large pot of lightly salted water to a boil. Cook macaroni in the boiling water, stirring occasionally until cooked through but firm to the bite, 8 minutes; drain and mix with chicken in the baking dish.
4. Melt 1/4 cup butter in a large pot over medium heat. Cook flour in melted butter until the flour is cooked and the mixture forms a roux, about 5 minutes. Stream milk into the pot while stirring to mix with the roux completely; cook until just about simmering, about 5 minutes more. Add Cheddar cheese in small amounts to the sauce and stir to melt completely before adding the next portion; cook and stir until thick and smooth, 2 to 3 minutes. Pour the sauce over the chicken and macaroni; stir to coat.
5. Melt 1/4 cup butter in the skillet in which you cooked the chicken over medium heat. Stir remaining tablespoon garlic powder into the melted butter; cook until fragrant, 1 to 2 minutes. Remove skillet from heat and stir crushed crackers into the butter mixture to coat; spread over the chicken and macaroni mixture in the baking dish.
6. Bake in preheated oven until the topping is crispy, 35 to 45 minutes.

BEE'S MAC AND CHEESE BAKE

Servings: 8 | Prep: 10m | Cooks: 57m | Total: 1h10m | Additional: 3m

NUTRITION FACTS

Calories: 541 | Carbohydrates: 56.9g | Fat: 23.7g | Protein: 24.1g | Cholesterol: 59mg

INGREDIENTS

- 1 (16 ounce) package uncooked pasta shells
- 1 (2.5 ounce) jar chopped pimentos, drained
- 1 (10.75 ounce) can condensed cream of mushroom soup
- 4 ounces soda crackers, crushed
- 1 (16 ounce) package shredded Cheddar cheese

DIRECTIONS

1. Preheat the oven to 350 degrees F (175 degrees C). Lightly grease a large casserole dish.
2. Bring a large pot of lightly salted water to a boil. Stir in shell pasta and cook 12 minutes, or until tender but still firm. Drain, and transfer to a large bowl.
3. Mix cream of mushroom soup, Cheddar cheese, and pimentos with the pasta. Pour into the prepared casserole dish. Top with crushed crackers.
4. Cover dish, and bake 30 minutes in the preheated oven. Remove cover, and continue baking 15 minutes, until cheese is bubbly and crackers are lightly browned.

EASY BAKED MAC-N-CHEESE

Servings: 8 | Prep: 10m | Cooks: 40m | Total: 50m

NUTRITION FACTS

Calories: 569 | Carbohydrates: 48.1g | Fat: 32.3g | Protein: 21.7g | Cholesterol: 70mg

INGREDIENTS

- 1 pound rotini pasta
- 1/4 cup bread crumbs, or more to taste
- 1 (16 ounce) jar Alfredo sauce
- 2 tablespoons shredded Cheddar cheese, or more to taste
- 3/4 pound shredded Cheddar cheese

DIRECTIONS

1. Preheat oven to 350 degrees F (175 degrees C).
2. Bring a large pot of lightly salted water to a boil; cook the rotini at a boil until tender yet firm to the bite, about 8 minutes; drain pasta and return to pot. Stir Alfredo sauce and 3/4 pound Cheddar cheese into pasta until cheese begins to melt. Pour pasta mixture into a 9x13-inch baking dish; top with bread crumbs and 2 tablespoons Cheddar cheese.

3. Bake in the preheated oven until cheese is melted and bread crumbs are golden brown, about 30 minutes.

MAC AND CHEESE IN A CHEESE WAFFLE CONE

Servings: 5 | Prep: 10m | Cooks: 15m | Total: 40m | Additional: 15m

NUTRITION FACTS

Calories: 381 | Carbohydrates: 28.5g | Fat: 23g | Protein: 15.4g | Cholesterol: 67mg

INGREDIENTS

- 5 ounces Cheddar cheese, finely grated
- 1/4 cup butter
- 1 (7.25 ounce) package macaroni and cheese mix
- 1 ounce sliced pepperoni
- 1/4 cup whole milk
- 1 teaspoon salt

DIRECTIONS

1. Preheat oven to 350 degrees F (175 degrees C). Line a baking sheet with parchment paper.
2. Sprinkle Cheddar cheese onto the prepared baking sheet.
3. Bake in the preheated oven until edges start to brown and cheese is bubbling, 5 to 10 minutes. Remove from oven and cool to room temperature. Cut melted cheese into squares and form into cones. Freeze cones for 5 minutes.
4. Bring a large pot of lightly salted water to a boil. Cook elbow macaroni in the boiling water, stirring occasionally until cooked through but firm to the bite, 8 minutes. Drain and return pasta to pot. Mix milk, butter, pepperoni, salt, and cheese packet into pasta until evenly combined.
5. Fill cheese cones with macaroni and cheese.

ED'S MACARONI JUMBLE

Servings: 4 | Prep: 15m | Cooks: 30m | Total: 45m

NUTRITION FACTS

Calories: 602 | Carbohydrates: 64.8g | Fat: 24.2g | Protein: 33.4g | Cholesterol: 83mg

INGREDIENTS

- 2 cups elbow macaroni
- 1/2 cup ketchup
- 2 teaspoons vegetable oil
- 1/2 cup water

- 1 pound lean ground beef
- 2 teaspoons chili powder
- 1/3 cup chopped onion
- 1/2 teaspoon white sugar
- 1 1/2 cups frozen corn
- 1/2 teaspoon seasoned salt
- 1 (6.5 ounce) can tomato sauce
- 1/2 cup grated Cheddar cheese

DIRECTIONS

1. Bring a large pot of lightly salted water to a boil. Cook elbow macaroni in the boiling water, stirring occasionally until cooked through but firm to the bite, 8 minutes. Drain.
2. Heat oil in a large pot over medium heat. Cook and stir beef and onion in the hot oil until beef is browned and crumbly, 5 to 7 minutes; drain and discard grease. Add corn, tomato sauce, ketchup, water, chili powder, sugar, and seasoned salt to the beef mixture; bring to a boil, reduce heat to medium-low, and simmer, stirring occasionally, until slightly thickened, about 10 minutes.
3. Stir macaroni into beef mixture; cook until heated through, about 5 minutes. Sprinkle with Cheddar cheese; remove from heat and let stand until cheese melts, 1 to 2 minutes.

SKINNY BROCCOLI MAC AND CHEESE
Servings: 10 | Prep: 10m | Cooks: 40m | Total: 50m

NUTRITION FACTS

Calories: 297.6 | Carbohydrates: 34.9g | Fat: 0g | Protein: 13.9g | Cholesterol: 33.7mg

INGREDIENTS

- 12 ounces high-fiber elbow macaroni (such as Ronzoni Smart Taste)
- 2 cups milk
- 1 (12 ounce) bag fresh broccoli florets
- 1 cup chicken broth
- 1 serving cooking spray
- 1 pinch salt and ground black pepper to taste
- 1 1/2 tablespoons butter
- 2 cups shredded sharp Cheddar cheese
- 1/4 cup minced onion
- 1/4 cup seasoned bread crumbs
- 1/4 cup all-purpose flour
- 2 tablespoons grated Parmesan cheese

DIRECTIONS

1. Bring a large pot of lightly salted water to a boil. Cook broccoli and elbow macaroni in the boiling water, stirring occasionally, until pasta is tender yet firm to the bite, about 8 minutes. Drain.
2. Preheat oven to 375 degrees F (190 degrees C). Spray a baking dish with cooking spray.
3. Melt butter in a large, heavy skillet over low heat. Add onion; cook and stir until slightly softened, about 2 minutes. Add flour; cook until golden and well combined, about 1 minute. Raise heat to medium-high. Whisk in milk and chicken broth and bring to a boil. Cook and stir until sauce is smooth and thick, about 5 minutes more. Season with salt and pepper. Remove from heat.
4. Stir Cheddar cheese into the sauce; add the cooked broccoli and macaroni. Mix well and pour into the prepared baking dish. Top with breadcrumbs and Parmesan cheese. Spray cooking spray on top.
5. Bake in the preheated oven until set, 15 to 20 minutes. Place under the broiler; cook until breadcrumbs are golden, about 3 minutes more.

MEMPHIS-STYLE CHICKEN MAC 'N CHEESE
Servings: 4 | Prep: 15m | Cooks: 35m | Total: 1h5m | Additional: 15m

NUTRITION FACTS

Calories: 665 | Carbohydrates: 36.6g | Fat: 36.9g | Protein: 48g | Cholesterol: 181mg

INGREDIENTS

- 1 tablespoon chili powder
- 2 1/2 cups cavatappi pasta, or similar shape such as rotini pasta
- 1 tablespoon dark brown sugar
- 2 tablespoons unsalted butter
- 1 teaspoon paprika
- 2 tablespoons all-purpose flour
- 1/2 teaspoon salt
- 1/2 cup chicken broth
- 1/2 teaspoon pepper
- 1 cup shredded extra-sharp orange Cheddar cheese
- 1/2 teaspoon garlic powder
- 1 cup shredded extra-sharp white Cheddar cheese
- 1/4 teaspoon cayenne pepper
- 1/2 teaspoon salt and pepper
- 1 1/2 pounds boneless skinless chicken thighs
- Reynolds Wrap Non-Stick Foil

DIRECTIONS

1. Preheat grill to medium-high.
2. Whisk all the ingredients for the Memphis-style rub in a small bowl and set aside.

3. Place 2 to 3 chicken thighs on a large 12x18-inch piece of Reynolds Wrap Non-Stick Foil. Generously sprinkle Memphis-style rub on all sides of the chicken, gently pressing it down.

4. Wrap up the chicken thighs in the foil. Repeat with the remaining chicken thighs.

5. Place foil-wrapped chicken thighs onto the grill.

6. Cover the grill and grill the chicken thighs for 15 to 20 minutes (longer or shorter depending on thickness of chicken) until tender and juices run clear or meat thermometer reads 165 degrees F. After the chicken is cooked through, carefully place the foil packet on a large plate. Carefully open foil with a pair of tongs and then, if desired, place chicken thighs directly onto grill to get nice grill marks and some char.

7. Let chicken thighs rest for 15 to 20 minutes or until cool enough to handle. Chop chicken into pieces.

8. Boil a pot of water, add the pasta and cook until al dente, about 10 to 12 minutes depending on the pasta shape you use. Drain.

9. Melt butter in a large skillet over medium-high heat. Whisk in flour and chicken broth. Let thicken for 3 to 5 minutes. Add cheeses to the skillet and stir with a spatula until melted and smooth.

10. Add the pasta to the cheese sauce and stir to incorporate.

11. Add the chicken pieces to the mac 'n cheese and stir to incorporate. Season with salt and pepper to taste.

PHILLY CHEESE STEAK PASTA

Servings: 6 | Prep: 20m | Cooks: 20m | Total: 40m

NUTRITION FACTS

Calories: 625 | Carbohydrates: 65.9g | Fat: 26.9g | Protein: 31.1g | Cholesterol: 72mg

INGREDIENTS

- 1 (16 ounce) box penne pasta
- 2 tablespoons butter, cut into small cubes
- 1/4 cup olive oil
- 2 tablespoons all-purpose flour
- 1 bell pepper, cut into strips
- 1 (12 ounce) can evaporated milk
- 1 medium onion, thinly sliced
- 1 clove garlic, minced
- 4 cloves garlic, minced
- 1/4 cup shredded sharp Cheddar cheese
- 1 pound beef top sirloin, thinly sliced
- 1/4 cup shredded Gouda cheese
- 1 teaspoon Italian seasoning
- 3 tablespoons grated Parmesan cheese

DIRECTIONS

1. Bring a large pot of lightly salted water to a boil. Add penne and cook, stirring occasionally, until tender yet firm to the bite, about 11 minutes.
2. Meanwhile, heat 2 tablespoons olive oil in a skillet over medium-high heat. Saute pepper, onion, and garlic for 3 minutes. Add steak and Italian seasoning. Saute until steak begins to firm and is hot and slightly pink in the center, 7 to 10 minutes more. Add remaining olive oil. Drain penne and mix into the skillet.
3. Melt butter in a saucepan over low heat. Whisk in flour; continue cooking and stirring until a paste forms, about 2 minutes. Add evaporated milk and garlic, stirring constantly until sauce is homogenous. Add Cheddar cheese and Gouda cheese by handfuls; continue stirring until completely melted, about 5 minutes. Remove sauce from heat and drizzle over the pasta.

BAKED CAULIFLOWER MACARONI & CHEESE
Servings: 5 | Prep: 5m | Cooks: 25m | Total: 30m

NUTRITION FACTS

Calories: 337 | Carbohydrates: 35.7g | Fat: 18.8g | Protein: 10.5g | Cholesterol: 52mg

INGREDIENTS

- Cooking spray
- 2 ounces cream cheese, at room temperature
- 1 1/2 cups bite-size cauliflower florets
- 1/3 cup shredded sharp white Cheddar cheese
- 1 (6 ounce) box Horizon ClassicMa Pasta Shells & White Cheddar Cheese
- 2/3 cup panko bread crumbs
- 4 tablespoons unsalted butter, divided
- 1/2 teaspoon salt
- 1/2 cup reduced fat milk
- 1/8 teaspoon ground black pepper

DIRECTIONS

1. Preheat oven to 375 degrees F (190 degrees C). Spray a ceramic or glass baking dish with cooking spray.
2. Bring a pot of water to a boil. Add cauliflower florets and boil for one minute. Remove with a slotted spoon.
3. Cook pasta shells in the same water, following instructions on the Horizon package. To the drained pasta, add 1/2 cup milk (instead of 1/4 cup as shown on the package), 2 tablespoons butter, and packet of cheese powder.
4. Stir in cream cheese and Cheddar cheese; mix well until combined and cheese is melted. Add cauliflower and mix. Season with salt and pepper, if desired.

5. Spoon macaroni and cheese into prepared baking dish. Smooth out the top.
6. Melt 2 tablespoons butter. In a small bowl, mix together panko breadcrumbs, melted butter, salt and pepper. Sprinkle over the top of the macaroni and cheese.
7. Bake until the breadcrumbs are golden brown, 15 to 17 minutes.

MACARONI AND CHEESE WITH SAUSAGE AND PEARS
Servings: 8 | Prep: 15m | Cooks: 50m | Total: 1h5m

NUTRITION FACTS

Calories: 443 | Carbohydrates: 36.9g | Fat: 24.4g | Protein: 19g | Cholesterol: 71mg

INGREDIENTS

- cooking spray
- 1/2 cup grated Parmesan cheese
- 1 (8 ounce) package elbow macaroni
- ground black pepper to taste
- 1/4 cup butter
- 1 (12 ounce) package fully-cooked sausage, sliced
- 1/4 onion, chopped
- 1 pear - peeled, cored, and sliced
- 2 1/2 tablespoons all-purpose flour, or as needed
- 2 tablespoons butter, melted
- 3 cups milk
- 1/2 cup bread crumbs
- 2 cups shredded sharp Cheddar cheese

DIRECTIONS

1. Preheat oven to 350 degrees F (175 degrees C). Spray a 3-quart casserole dish with cooking spray.
2. Bring a large pot of lightly salted water to a boil. Cook elbow macaroni in the boiling water, stirring occasionally until cooked through but firm to the bite, 8 minutes. Drain macaroni and transfer to the prepared casserole dish.
3. Heat butter in a saucepan over medium heat; cook and stir onions in the melted butter until partially translucent, about 5 minutes. Whisk in flour until paste-like consistency, 3 to 5 minutes. Slowly stream in milk, stirring constantly, until flour mixture is incorporated, about 5 minutes. Stir in Cheddar cheese and Parmesan cheese until completely melted and and sauce has thickened, 5 to 10 minutes.
4. Pour cheese sauce into macaroni; stir to coat. Season with black pepper. Stir in sausage.
5. Reserve 4 slices of pears; dice remaining pear slices and stir into macaroni mixture. Arrange the reserved slices atop macaroni mixture.

6. Stir 2 tablespoons melted butter and bread crumbs together in a small bowl; sprinkle over macaroni mixture.
7. Bake in the preheated oven until cheese is bubbling and topping is lightly browned, about 30 minutes.

CHEDDAR AND VEGETABLE PASTA BAKE

Servings: 4 | Prep: 25m | Cooks: 17m | Total: 42m

NUTRITION FACTS

Calories: 465 | Carbohydrates: 48.3g | Fat: 19.2g | Protein: 28.6g | Cholesterol: 59mg

INGREDIENTS

- 2 tablespoons butter or margarine
- 1/2 teaspoon hot pepper sauce (optional)
- 2 cloves garlic, minced
- 2 cups Sargento Shredded Reduced Fat Mild Cheddar Cheese, divided
- 1 1/2 tablespoons flour
- 1 (16 ounce) package frozen mixed vegetables (cauliflower, red bell peppers, broccoli), thawed
- 1 (12 fluid ounce) can evaporated skim milk
- 3 cups bow tie or penne pasta, cooked and drained
- 3/4 teaspoon salt

DIRECTIONS

1. Melt butter in large saucepan over medium heat. Add garlic; cook 2 minutes. Add flour; cook and stir 1 minute. Add milk, salt and pepper sauce. Heat to a boil, stirring constantly. Remove from heat; stir in 1 cup cheese until melted.
2. Add sauce and vegetables to pasta; toss well. Transfer to a greased medium baking dish or oval casserole. Cover with foil; bake in preheated 375 degrees F oven 15 minutes or until hot. Uncover and sprinkle with remaining cheese; bake 2 minutes more or until cheese is melted.

MACARONI WITH WHITE SAUCE

Servings: 12 | Prep: 45m | Cooks: 30m | Total: 1h15m

NUTRITION FACTS

Calories: 536 | Carbohydrates: 55.2g | Fat: 20.8g | Protein: 30.3g | Cholesterol: 63mg

INGREDIENTS

- 1 1/2 (16 ounce) packages uncooked elbow macaroni
- ground black pepper to taste

- 2 tablespoons vegetable oil, divided
- 1/4 cup vegetable oil
- 2 cubes chicken bouillon
- 3/4 cup all-purpose flour
- 1 large onion, chopped
- 3 cups milk
- 1 3/4 pounds ground beef
- 1/2 teaspoon ground white pepper
- 4 tablespoons tomato paste
- 3 cups shredded mozzarella cheese
- salt to taste

DIRECTIONS

1. Preheat oven to 350 degrees F (175 degrees C). Grease a 9x13 inch baking dish.
2. Bring a large pot of lightly salted water to a boil. Add pasta, 1 tablespoon oil and bouillon cubes, and cook for 8 to 10 minutes or until al dente; drain.
3. Heat 1 tablespoon oil in a large skillet. Saute onion until golden and add ground beef. Cook over medium heat until evenly brown. Stir in tomato paste, salt and pepper; simmer over low heat until heated through.
4. Heat 1/4 cup oil in a deep saucepan; stir in flour, then milk. Cook over medium-low heat until sauce thickens; stir in salt and white pepper. Pour half of the sauce over the cooked macaroni and stir in mozzarella cheese. Spoon half of the macaroni into prepared dish and top with ground beef mixture. Spoon the remaining macaroni over the ground beef, and top with remaining white sauce.
5. Bake in preheated oven for 30 minutes, or until golden brown.

CHEEZY MACARONI AND LITTLE SMOKIES

Servings: 8 | Prep: 5m | Cooks: 20m | Total: 25m

NUTRITION FACTS

Calories: 530 | Carbohydrates: 52g | Fat: 25.8g | Protein: 21.2g | Cholesterol: 62mg

INGREDIENTS

- 1 (16 ounce) package elbow macaroni
- 1 (16 ounce) package little smokie sausages
- 1 (10.75 ounce) can condensed Cheddar cheese soup
- 8 ounces processed cheese, cubed
- 1 cup milk
- 1 cup frozen diced carrots
- 2 tablespoons dried minced onion flakes

DIRECTIONS

1. Fill a large pot with lightly salted water, bring to a boil, and stir in the macaroni. Return to a boil and cook the pasta uncovered, stirring occasionally, until cooked through but still firm to the bite, about 8 minutes. Drain well.
2. Whisk together the soup, milk, and onion flakes in a large saucepan over medium-low heat. Bring to a simmer, and stir in the sausage links, cheese, and carrots. Bring the mixture back to a boil, stirring frequently, until the cheese has melted and the mixture is bubbling.
3. Stir in the hot cooked macaroni, and serve.

HEALTHIER FOUR CHEESE MACARONI
Servings: 6 | Prep: 25m | Cooks: 35m | Total: 1h

NUTRITION FACTS

Calories: 591 | Carbohydrates: 61g | Fat: 27.7g | Protein: 24.7g | Cholesterol: 137mg

INGREDIENTS

- 1 (16 ounce) package elbow macaroni
- 1/2 cup shredded part-skim mozzarella cheese
- 1/2 cup butter
- 8 ounces evaporated milk
- 1/2 cup shredded reduced-fat Cheddar cheese
- 2 eggs, beaten
- 1/2 cup shredded Jarlsberg cheese
- 1/4 teaspoon salt
- 1/2 cup shredded reduced-fat Monterey Jack cheese
- 1/8 teaspoon ground black pepper

DIRECTIONS

1. Preheat oven to 350 degrees F (175 degrees C). Lightly grease a deep 2 1/2-quart baking dish.
2. Bring a large pot of lightly salted water to a boil. Cook elbow macaroni in boiling water, stirring occasionally until cooked through but firm to the bite, 8 minutes. Drain and return to cooking pot.
3. Melt butter in a small saucepan over medium heat. Stir into macaroni.
4. Combine Cheddar, Jarlsberg, Monterey Jack, and mozzarella cheeses in a large bowl; mix well. Add evaporated milk, 1 1/2 cups cheese mixture, and eggs to macaroni. Mix together and season with salt and ground pepper. Transfer to baking dish and sprinkle with remaining cheese mixture.
5. Bake in preheated oven until hot and bubbling around the edges, about 25 minutes.

ONE-PAN CHEDDAR MAC
Servings: 4 | Prep: 5m | Cooks: 20m | Total: 25m

NUTRITION FACTS

Calories: 438 | Carbohydrates: 44g | Fat: 19.1g | Protein: 21g | Cholesterol: 55mg

INGREDIENTS

- 3 cups College Inn Chicken Broth
- Crumbled cooked bacon
- 8 ounces elbow macaroni
- Steamed broccoli florets
- 6 ounces shredded sharp Cheddar cheese
- Chopped fresh tomatoes
- 1/4 cup reduced-fat cream cheese or low-fat Greek yogurt
- Sliced green onion
- Ground black pepper, to taste

DIRECTIONS

1. Bring broth to a boil in a large saucepan; add macaroni and reduce heat to medium-high. Cook according to package directions, stirring frequently. DO NOT DRAIN.
2. Remove from heat; stir in cheeses and black pepper, if desired, until cheese is melted.

BAKED TOMATO MAC 'N CHEESE

Servings: 6 | Prep: 1h | Cooks: 30m | Total: 1h30m

NUTRITION FACTS

Calories: 703 | Carbohydrates: 10.6g | Fat: 33.7g | Protein: 29g | Cholesterol: 96mg

INGREDIENTS

- 1 (16 ounce) package elbow macaroni
- 16 ounces shredded Colby-Monterey Jack cheese
- 4 tablespoons butter
- 1 (14.5 ounce) can Hunt's Diced Tomatoes, drained
- 1 cup milk
- 2 (7 ounce) cans salsa verde
- 3 tablespoons flour
- ground black pepper to taste

DIRECTIONS

1. Preheat oven to 375 degrees F (190 degrees C).
2. Bring a large pot of lightly salted water to a boil. Cook elbow macaroni in the boiling water, stirring occasionally until tender yet firm to the bite, 8 minutes. Drain.

3. Whisk milk and flour together in a small bowl.

4. Melt butter in a large heavy pot over medium heat. Pour in milk/flour mixture; stir constantly until thickened. Add most of the cheese, reserving a few tablespoons to sprinkle over top before baking. Mix in drained tomatoes, and salsa verde. Continue stirring until cheese is melted. Season to taste with black pepper. Stir in macaroni and thoroughly blend with the sauce.

5. Divide among individual serving-sized ovenproof baking dishes or ramekins. Top with remaining cheese. and bake 10 minutes. Place under broiler for an additional 3-5 minutes, or until top is browned.

6. Bake in preheated oven until hot and bubbly, about 10 minutes. Turn on the broiler and cook until tops are browned, about 2 to 3 minutes.

BLENDER MACARONI AND CHEESE

Servings: 6 | Prep: 20m | Cooks: 40m | Total: 1h

NUTRITION FACTS

Calories: 469 | Carbohydrates: 49.1g | Fat: 19.4g | Protein: 23.8g | Cholesterol: 58mg

INGREDIENTS

- 2/3 pound uncooked elbow macaroni
- 1/4 teaspoon black pepper
- 10 ounces extra-sharp Cheddar cheese, cubed
- 1/2 teaspoon salt
- 1 1/2 cups hot milk
- 1/2 teaspoon dry mustard powder
- 1/4 cup all-purpose flour
- 1 pinch garlic powder
- 1/2 small onion, cut into chunks
- 1/4 cup toasted wheat germ
- 1 tablespoon Worcestershire sauce
- 1/4 cup grated Parmesan cheese

DIRECTIONS

1. Preheat oven to 350 degrees F (175 degrees C). Butter a 2-quart casserole dish.

2. Bring a large pot of lightly salted water to a boil. Add macaroni and cook for 8 to 10 minutes or until al dente; drain well and pour into prepared casserole dish.

3. Meanwhile, place the Cheddar cheese, hot milk, flour, onion, Worcestershire sauce, pepper, salt, mustard powder, and garlic powder in the bowl of a blender. Blend until cheese is melted and onion is finely chopped.

4. Pour cheese mixture over macaroni. Sprinkle top with wheat germ and Parmesan cheese. Bake uncovered for 30 minutes.